Chèvre!
THE GOAT CHEESE COOKBOOK

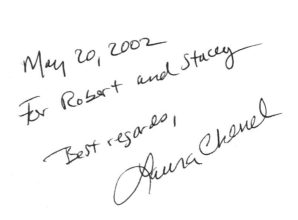

May 20, 2002
For Robert and Stacey

Best regards,
Laura Chenel

Chèvre!

THE GOAT CHEESE
C O O K B O O K

LAURA CHENEL • LINDA SIEGFRIED

Aris Books

▲
▼▼

Addison-Wesley Publishing Company, Inc.
Reading, Massachusetts   Menlo Park, California   New York
Don Mills, Ontario   Wokingham, England   Amsterdam
Bonn   Sydney   Singapore   Tokyo   Madrid   San Juan

Library of Congress Cataloging-in-Publication Data

Chenel, Laura.
     Chèvre! : the goat cheese cookbook / Laura Chenel, Linda
Siegfried.
     p.   cm.
     ISBN 0-201-52383-3
     1. Cookery (Goat cheese)   I. Siegfried, Linda.   II. Title.
TX759.5.C48C5   1990
641.6'73 — dc20   89-29124

Aris Books Editorial Offices and Test Kitchen
1621 Fifth Street
Berkeley, CA 94710
(415) 527-5171

Cover design by Copenhaver Cumpston
Cover photograph by Mark Adams
Text design by Carol Denison & Co.
Illustrated by Patricia Waters

   BCDEFGHIJ-VB-954
First printing, February 1990

ACKNOWLEDGEMENTS

We wish to thank many people for helping us with this book. To begin, a hearty thanks to the following people for taking time to taste and test: Zara Altair, Gretchen Cooper, Rachel Helm, Otis Holt, Lorin Leith, Danielle Murray, Bretta Rambo, Nick Rettinghouse, John Simmons, Carl and Kathy Vast, John Wright; and we are particularly grateful to Barbara Backus, Kaye and Larry Henzerling, Roland Jacopetti, Patti Traulsen and Jeanne Woods for their additional assistance and suggestions. Also, thanks to all the people who took five minutes or two hours to discuss the project with us.

We are especially indebted to Cynthia Pawlcyn for contributing her original recipes, for testing a large number of our recipes and for so generously sharing her professional expertise; and to Scottie McKinney for her original recipes and her untiring experimentation with goat cheese cooking. Also, many thanks to our other contributing chefs: Larry Forgione, Wolfgang Puck, Alice Waters and Jonathan Waxman.

We wish to give special thanks to Dorothy Foster Sly for her contribution of the section on nutrition and for her invaluable editorial assistance; to Carol Denison for her sound advice and for the beauty of her design; and to Mark Adams for his enthusiasm, his generosity and his elegant photographs. Were it not for the pushing, prompting, and support of these three people, we might still be writing this book.

With much gratitude and affection we thank Fred and Silvie Vast (Laurie's parents) for their unflagging assistance, support and ideas; and James Rettinghouse, the person who inspired us to begin this project.

CONTENTS

INTRODUCTION

It comes in cylinders, pyramids, ovals, and logs; wrapped in chestnut and grape leaves; pierced with a straw or stick, like a popsicle; marinated in oil or brandy; or coated with ash, pepper, and fragrant herbs. Sometimes sweet, sometimes salty, it is sold creamy and fresh, or firm and long-aged. It is both a rare culinary treat and a dietary staple. Such is the versatility of cheese made from the milk of goats.

In Greece it is popular as salty feta; in Norway, as whey-sweet Gjetost; in Italy, as the family of cheeses, Formaggio di Capra; in France as silken-rich chèvre (pronounced shev). And in the United States, goat cheese, which is made here in a creamy, fresh style similar to the French chèvre, is only now becoming known. It was in 1981 that the first commercial chèvre-style goat cheese plant, Laura Chenel's Chèvre, was established, despite the fact that the milk-plentiful goat arrived in America along with the Puritans.

Since long before the landing at Plymouth these nimble, independent creatures have scrambled and foraged the rocky precipices of mountainous regions of the world. Intelligent, affectionate, and highly productive, they serve man well. From the earliest civilizations on, food providers have capitalized on the goat's ability to survive on sparse vegetation not suitable for larger, less agile livestock. Today the goat is the most common farm animal found around the world.

In spite of long domestication, true taming of this innately mischievious animal will likely never be possible. More important, however, than the day-to-day trials of goat keeping, are the wealth of goods the goat provides in her hide, horns, and milk—and ultimately from her milk—in cheese.

Cheeses of all varieties, including goat, have been an integral part of the human diet for over 5000 years. But the craft of cheesemaking has always been considered somewhat of a mystery. The secrets of the process have been passed from generation to generation within many cultures of the world. A vast array of distinctive cheese styles has evolved,

1

each influenced by the climate, topography, and social customs of the region in which it is made. A fact perhaps no better illustrated than by world-wide differences in goat cheese.

In the United States, the turning of goat milk into curds and whey has been limited, until recently, to a family endeavor. Cow milk cheeses, on the other hand, have been made commercially in the U.S. since the mid-nineteenth century. The industrial revolution, which occurred shortly thereafter, encouraged mass production and distribution of food products. And Velveeta was quickly established as the then state-of-the-art American cheese.

Americans seeking more than mass-produced flavor in foods have always enjoyed access to a wide variety of ethnic restaurants—thanks to our melting-pot heritage. But, outside of regional specialties, our "American Food" has not reflected ethnic influences, and a stylized cuisine has been slow to develop.

Since World War II popular interest in foods has broadened dramatically. Americans have traveled overseas, sampling widely in foreign cuisines. Improved trade and transport systems have made much of the world's bounty available through local supermarkets. And more immediately, Americans have become concerned about food quality and good nutrition.

Since the early 1960's, what began as a back-to-the-land movement has matured to an enduring preference for more natural foods. American tastes are changing. Consumers now demand simplicity, freshness, and diversity in food products. In response, a host of new specialty food stores and supermarket departments have emerged in urban and rural communities. Regional farmers' markets are proliferating and thriving.

Almost simultaneously, a profusion of innovative young professional chefs have taken command of restaurant kitchens. Learning techniques of many cultures (particularly European and Asian), and adopting the tenets of freshness and simplicity, they have developed a new version of American food.

Today a meal in an American restaurant may be presented in the crisp styling of the Japanese, and yet be redolent with the herbs of Italy, or flavored subtly in the tradition of the French. The ingredients? Primarily whatever is local and in season.

While professional chefs may seem the leaders in changing American cuisine, home cooks, too, are showing great imagination. In kitchens across the country, fresh foods from the marketplace and garden are being combined in new ways, and the stock sauces are more apt to be hoisin and salsa than catsup and sweet relish.

Indeed, it is vigorous appreciation for the role of experimentation in cooking, and the advent of American-produced goat cheese, which led to the creation of this cookbook. We present this introduction to goat cheese cooking in a toast to the increasing sophistication of the American palate, and to the creativity and enthusiasm of the home cook.

You will find here recipes which incorporate goat cheese in familiar fare, as well as others which might seem more unusual combinations of foods. The recipes are ours, adaptations of others', and the contributions of some of the most exciting chefs in this country—Larry Forgione, Wolfgang Puck, Alice Waters, and Jonathan Waxman.

We hope that you will enjoy these selections, and that you will find them not only a pleasure to the palate, but inspiration for culinary creations of your own.

THE MAKING OF FRESH GOAT CHEESE, CALIFORNIA CHÈVRE STYLE

Making fresh goat cheese is amazingly simple. Unlike most other cheeses the procedure involves no heating of curds, no pressing of whey from curds, and just a modest amount of aging time.

There are three essentials to the process: impeccably clean, fresh milk; attention to detail; and constant observation. This third component might also be called the cheesemaker's skill. For the professional, cheesemaking is, more than anything else, a private rhythm and compelling involvement with a special world—the miracle of the transformation of milk to cheese.

Of the three essentials to cheesemaking, milk quality is the most significant. The milk must be the freshest available, and it must be clean. A delicious, high-quality cheese cannot be produced from inferior milk. The milk, then, is the bottom line.

Surprisingly, this critical ingredient, the milk, is 7/8ths water. The milk's protein, sugar (lactose), fat, vitamins, minerals, and trace elements are concentrated in a small quantity of solids suspended in the water. In cheesemaking it is a component of the milk protein, casein, which is of concern. Casein is the substance that is "curdled"— the process during which the formerly flexible protein strands take on a new, rigid shape.

Attention to detail, the second ingredient in the cheesemaking process, pertains particularly to cleanliness in the cheesemaking environment. The milk must be sanitary. And workers, utensils, and the cheesemaking area all must be contaminant-free.

This attention to detail must continue throughout the multi-phase cheesemaking process. First the milk is warmed to 75-85°F to provide an environment hospitable to the milk sugar-loving lactic acid bacteria. The bacteria are added to the milk in a cheese "starter culture." The warm temperature activates the bacteria, and they feed on the milk's lactose sugar, turning it into lactic acid.

An acid environment is necessary to the next step in cheesemaking—addition of the curdling agent, rennet. Acidity promotes curdling, helps expel the liquid whey, stems the growth of undesirable bacteria, and adds to the flavor of the cheese.

Rennets of both animal and vegetable extract are used to coagulate milk. In the past the most commonly used rennet was a substance taken from the stomach lining of a nursing calf or kid goat. Other coagulants have been produced from plants, including the thistle, stinging nettle, and fig tree. But the most common commercial coagulant in America is derived from a pure culture of the bacteria *Mucor miehei*.

Following the addition of coagulant the goat milk is allowed to sit undisturbed for 8 to 30 hours. During this period the casein protein curdles and soft cheese curds form.

Once the desired consistency is reached the curds are gently ladled into molds of various shapes and sizes (logs, pyramids, disks, etc.). The curds remain in the molds for approximately 24 hours, becoming firmer as more whey drains out. Next, the young cheeses are turned out of the molds, lightly salted, and placed on curing trays.

The trays are then arranged in a temperature- and humidity-controlled drying room, where they remain for three to four days. Each cheese is turned daily to ensure even draining and curing. When the cheeses have achieved optimum firmness, dryness, texture and flavor, and have begun to develop a light yellow crust, they are removed from the drying room.

At this point, the cheese is ready to eat. Its flavor will be mild and fresh. Most American-made goat cheese is offered at this fresh stage, either plain or coated with various herbs or spices.

The third essential ingredient in the cheesemaking process—constant care and observation on the part of the cheesemaker—must be practiced from the start. From this constancy emerges a "feeling" for the cheese. Eventually, the alert cheesemaker knows the condition of the cheese by the odor of the room, by the way the cheese feels in the hand, and by the way it appears at a glance. The development of this "sixth sense" for the health of the cheese is the professional's skill.

Finally, it is important to note some of the many transient factors which may affect cheesemaking. For example, grasses and herbs eaten by the goats may influence milk flavor; and the time of year, atmospheric conditions, climate, quality of water—even mood of the cheesemaker—all contribute to the quality of the final product. Just as no two goats will produce milk that tastes the same, no two cheesemakers will match in technique, and no two goat cheeses will have identical flavor. The variety is endless— and endlessly fascinating.

ON GOAT CHEESE AND NUTRITION

Goat cheese is certainly good tasting food, but does it provide good nutrition? The answer is a definite "Yes."

Lower in calories and easier to digest than many other cheeses, chèvre contains significant amounts of protein, vitamins, and minerals. A three-ounce portion of fresh goat cheese—an amount that might be consumed at lunch with French bread and fruit—supplies the average female about 30 percent of her daily requirement for protein (RDA) and just 246 calories. Men have higher protein requirements, and a three-ounce portion of cheese supplies 25 percent of their RDA for the nutrient.

The high digestibility of goat cheese results from the unusual structure of its component fats. The fats in goat cheese and milk are generally small molecules made up of short-chain fatty acids. Their small size makes them easier to break down and digest than the larger long-chain fats of cow milk and cheese.

Goat milk and cow milk are similar in calcium and phosphorus mineral contents. Goat milk, however, has greater quantities of potassium, vitamin A, thiamin, and niacin. Chèvre lacks folacin (folic acid) and vitamin B-12; cow milk is a major source of these two vitamins in the human diet.

So, while the rich flavor of goat cheese pleases the palate and nourishes the soul, chèvre also refuels the body with a variety of essential nutrients.

Here's a brief comparison of goat milk cheese and cow milk cheeses in terms of macronutrients and sodium:

per ounce	calories	grams protein	grams fat	grams carbo-hydrate	milli-grams sodium	milli-grams choles-terol
Fresh goat cheese	82	4.5	6.8	0.9	180	20
Cheddar	114	7.1	9.4	0.4	176	30
Cream cheese	99	2.1	9.9	0.6	84	31
Brie	95	5.9	7.9	0.1	178	28
Parmesan, grated	129	11.8	8.5	1.1	528	22

BUYING AND STORING CHÈVRE

Buying chèvre, or goat cheese, is an adventure—there are so many varieties from which to choose. In France, where cheesemaking is a revered art, there are at least 60 subtly different regional chèvres. Many of these cheeses reach our shores. But goat cheese production in the United States is increasing, too. There are over fifty goat cheese makers in the U.S.

Fresh chèvre is a soft cheese. It is made by a curdling process more gentle than the process used in production of most hard cheeses. Because of this, chèvre has a high moisture content—up to 60 percent of total weight. Much of this moisture is whey, a protein-containing liquid.

Fresh chèvres' high moisture content spells a relatively short shelf life for the cheese. This is true for all soft cheeses—all ferment easily, quickly develop exterior mold, and grow strong in aroma and flavor.

This high perishability means that you should carefully choose the merchant from whom you will buy your goat cheese. Find a competent, knowledgeable shopkeeper who will allow you to taste cheeses and who will answer your questions. Look for a clean, orderly—but busy—shop with a regular turnover of product. This combination of factors is some insurance that the cheeses will be in good condition. Also, note how the cheeses are cared for. For example, they should not be stored near meats because they readily absorb the aromas and flavors of stronger foods.

When buying a "fresh" cheese, make sure it *is* fresh. If in doubt, ask for a sample; the cheese should have no odor of ammonia and no sour taste.

Fresh chèvre is generally sold wrapped in Cryovac, a thick plastic that allows for a relatively long shelf life. However, you may find some chèvres wrapped in plastic film. Occasionally the film causes a skin to develop between the cheese and the plastic. This does not indicate spoilage and does not harm the cheese; simply remove with the aid of a knife.

Do not confuse fresh chèvre with varieties inoculated with a *Penicillium* mold, such as bucheron, taupinière, and some versions of crottin. These cheeses develop a downy white exterior and a sharp, piquant flavor as they age. They should be wrapped first in paper, then over-wrapped in plastic. It is best not to wrap them directly in plastic, as this is harmful to their white mold.

To some extent tight wrapping preserves cheese, but it is also essential to keep cheese cool. Store fresh chèvres in the coldest section of your refrigerator, where the low temperature will minimize potential growth of bacteria.

Remember that all cheeses are affected by fluctuations in temperature and humidity and by exposure to air or sunlight. The full integrity of a cheese is maintained only by careful storage.

If, by chance, you want to further age a cheese to encourage development of a more pronounced flavor, store the cheese in a warmer section of your refrigerator (i.e. the butter compartment), loosely wrapped in wax paper. The ideal temperature for this is 45-50°F; a wine cellar might be the perfect spot.

To store a cheese that has been cut and partially consumed, wrap tightly in plastic film or aluminum foil. This will prevent loss of moisture and consequent drying. Should mold develop on the surface of the cheese, don't throw the cheese away. Taste it. The mold is edible and you may enjoy its unusual flavor. Likewise, a cheese that has mistakenly been allowed to dry out can be a great addition to a salad or sauce.

For more lengthy storage you might consider freezing chèvre. As long as the cheese is in good condition and tightly wrapped (in either plastic film or aluminum foil), its flavor, texture, and moisture content will remain unchanged.

Freeze the cheese in small packages—in quantities of one pound or less. Larger pieces freeze slowly and the extended process can damage the cheese, causing it to crumble when thawed. Remember to thaw chèvre slowly. Leave it undisturbed in the refrigerator for a period of 24-48 hours.

Finally, for fullest cheese flavor and eating pleasure, be sure to remove chèvre (and all other cheeses) from the refrigerator at least one hour before serving.

CHEESE AS A COURSE

Cheese, in America, has been considered simply an optional ingredient in sandwiches and sauces. By contrast, in Europe it is traditional to serve cheese as a separate course during daily meals. The European cheese course commonly follows the main course and salad, preceding dessert. Occasionally cheese is offered with salad, instead of salad, or in place of dessert.

There is more to this custom than mere appreciation for the good taste of cheese: cheese is an effective aid to digestion. Because it is mostly protein, it is a potent stimulant to the production of digestive juices and can help to quickly ease that full-stomach feeling.

Likewise, cheese served immediately following the salad course cleanses the mouth of residual acids from the salad dressing. Thus, the palate is refreshed, the tastebuds readied for the sensation of dessert. Alternately, a cheese course can provide the perfect occasion for finishing the dinner wine (or can act, perhaps, as an excuse for opening another bottle).

In fact, many cheese lovers choose to end their meal with a simple dessert of cheese and wine. Fresh fruits—such as grapes, apples, and pears—dried figs and nuts, or even bread and butter, are excellent accompaniments. One of our favorite dessert combinations is fresh goat cheese with warmed cracked walnuts and a well-aged port.

Wines and cheeses tend to heighten each other's already complex flavors. Sometimes they work as perfect complements, smoothing out rough flavor characteristics or bringing out a nuance of taste. As a general rule, serve light wines with mild cheeses and more robust wines with stronger cheeses.

We find that goat cheese pairs successfully with a wide variety of wines. A chèvre course might be accented well by wines such as: French Burgundy or Bordeaux, French or

California Sauvignon Blanc, California Chardonnay, or California Cabernet Sauvignon. But the mating of wine and cheese is a subjective endeavour; we recommend (endless) experimentation as the best way to discover personal favorites.

To facilitate experimentation, when serving a cheese course, offer a variety of at least three or four kinds of cheese. Present them in an attractive manner, on a wood board, a slab of marble, or a large ceramic serving platter. A variety of goat cheeses—some tangy and fresh, others peppery and long-aged—may be all the diversity needed. However, chèvres complement many other types of cheese, so you may want to include a Swiss, Blue, Camembert, or a triple crème in your selection. Accompany with a basket of crusty bread or unsalted crackers.

Remember that for fullest flavor, cheese must be allowed to reach room temperature before eating; an hour out of the refrigerator is usually sufficient time. Set out only the amount of cheese you expect to be consumed. This protects the bulk of the cheese from unnecessary exposure to air and warm temperatures.

When slicing cheese, try to preserve the integrity of the shape: pyramides should be cut in quarters, logs in slices, the others in wedges. A small fork can be a big help transporting cut pieces from the serving board to the plate.

Should you cut off and discard the rind? Not necessarily. The rind is not harmful, but it does have a flavor distinctly different from the rest of the cheese. If you enjoy its taste, go ahead and eat it.

Finally, when planning a cheese course, consider the balance of foods on the menu. Cheese is a rich food; a cheese course in a meal with other creamy or cheesy dishes might be over-kill. Likewise, cheese served in unlimited quantities as an hors d'oeuvre can dull the appetite.

DESCRIPTION OF CHEESES USED
IN THESE RECIPES

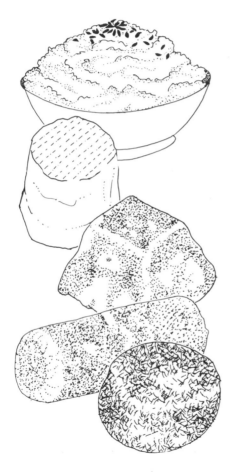

FROMAGE BLANC (fro mäge bläng)
Day-old curds whipped to a fluffy consistency;
light, creamy, fresh taste and texture.

FROMAGE BLANC, HERB
Fromage blanc with the addition of garlic and
freshly cut herbs.

CHABIS (shä bee)
Young, fresh, and mild; packaged at less than one
week old. Five-ounces, cylindrical shape.

PYRAMIDE
Cured a little longer than chabis. Usually ash-
coated and made in an 8-ounce pyramid shape.

LOG
Aged approximately one week; 1-1/2″ diameter
ashed or white log shape weighing 8 ounces.

PEPPER, HERB, DILL, etc.
Young when wrapped. Round, flat, 5-ounce
cheeses coated with various herbs.

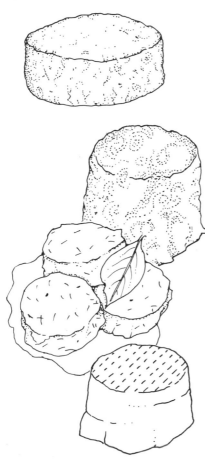

CALISTOGAN
Aged ten days to two weeks before wrapping. Dense, creamy texture and full flavor; 2-1/2 ounces each.

TAUPINIÈRE (toe pee nyair)
A "molehill" shaped cheese, aged three weeks. The ashed exterior is sprayed with white *Penicillium* mold, producing a more pronounced, complex flavor; 9 ounces.

CABECOU (kä bā koo)
Button-like 1-ounce cheeses cured two to three weeks, then marinated in California olive oil and herbs. Pleasing nutty flavor and drier texture.

CROTTIN (kro tan)
Aged two to three weeks. Downy white from its *Penicillium* mold, with a sharp, pronounced goat flavor and a dry texture; 2-1/2 to 3 ounces.

HINTS FOR USE OF GOAT CHEESE IN COOKING

Eating well doesn't necessarily demand spending a lot of time in the kitchen—and for us it can't. We're both full time business people. We both try to have large gardens, and we have many interests other than cooking.

The dishes we selected to present in this cookbook reflect our busy lifestyles. Most of the recipes are simple to prepare, yet are complex in flavor. The key: fresh, high quality ingredients and a little forethought.

You may find us somewhat provincial in our choice of ingredients. We are Californians; we developed and tested these recipes with Laura Chenel's Chèvre cheeses, and we drink mostly California wine. Naturally, you need not follow suit. But, if you must or if you choose to use imported cheese, please bear these thoughts in mind:

- Domestic cheese is generally fresher than imported cheese. This may affect the taste of your preparations as goat cheese tends to develop a stronger flavor as it ages.

- French and Italian cheeses tend to be saltier than their domestic versions. Taste your dishes as you go along, and be particularly careful when recipes call for adding salt.

- French fromage blanc usually contains more whey than the domestic; drain it for a couple of hours in a sieve lined with wet cheese cloth. Note that some recipes call for drained fromage blanc whether you use the domestic or imported variety.

Also, because fromage blanc is a very fresh and fairly delicate cheese, it should be used with care. If you whip it in a processor or blender, be quick so that the cheese will not turn to liquid.

All cheeses are heat sensitive. Goat cheese becomes grainy and separates when overheated. Many of our recipe instructions advise "do not allow to overcook," or "heat until just melted." It is well worth it to take the extra caution.

The recipe ingredient lists use a set format regarding the cheese. For example:

5 ounces chèvre (chabis), crumbled.

We have chosen to measure amounts by ounces rather than cups because this reflects the way cheeses are sold, and the size of the units readily available. For example, Laura Chenel's Chèvre chabis weighs 5 ounces, pyramides weigh 8 ounces, etc. Therefore, if a recipe calls for 2 ounces of a cheese, it would amount to 1/4 of a pyramide, or a little more than 1/3 of a chabis. Remember, too, that the measure of cheese need not be exact. Feel free to increase or lessen the amount as your budget allows or palate suggests. Also, the parentheses surrounding "chabis" indicates it is the type of cheese suggested for the recipe—not the absolute. Note that in all recipes—and throughout the book—the words chèvre and goat cheese are used interchangeably.

OTHER INGREDIENTS

We prefer to use fresh, in-season ingredients—herbs, fruits, vegetables, cheese—in all preparations. Obviously, this is not always possible. Our remedies are freezing and home canning.

For example, vine-ripened tomatoes can easily and safely be canned at home. They also freeze well—just peel and core, squeeze out some of the seeds, pack in zip-lock bags, and freeze. Of course, frozen tomatoes are not suitable for stuffing, but they work well in most cooked preparations.

For fresh ingredients out of season, look to specialty food stores. You might, however, want to consider what a beautiful peach or other food may have had to go through to be in the market in January.

Some of the ingredients used in our recipes are items that you may find only in specialty food stores. We have chosen to include these foods as ingredients because they contribute unique flavors and aromas. If some of these products are new to you, we encourage you to seek them out for use in these recipes—as well as for the new twist they may lend to old recipe favorites.

Of course, in a pinch, you can substitute what you have on hand for these special ingredients. For example, delicately-flavored sherry, raspberry, or champagne vinegars may be replaced with other vinegars. Where we suggest virgin olive oil (because we like its characteristic fruity taste), a less-than-virgin oil will do. And in recipes calling for peppery, spicy Italian prosciutto, another type of ham will suffice.

However, we can think of no suitable substitute for dried tomatoes, either preserved in olive oil or simply dried, ready to be easily and quickly reconstituted in hot water. Nor do we think there's a fair replacement for the tender Niçoise or meaty Greek olives, both of which are brine-cured and supremely flavorful.

A word on herbs: we prefer them fresh. There is one exception—oregano—which seems to have more potent flavor when dried. If all you have is fresh, toast before using.

In most instructions we suggest a specific quantity of fresh herbs to use and also list the appropriate substitute amount of dried herbs. The preferred is listed first:

    1 tablespoon fresh thyme or 1/2 tablespoon dried.

If only the fresh is mentioned, it is best not to substitute.

For example, in most recipes calling for basil we recommend using only the fresh. If obtaining fresh basil year 'round is as difficult for you as it is for us, we have a solution. During the summer, when your garden or local market is full of the fragrant, silky leaves, finely chop a bunch in a blender or processor. Add a little lemon juice and/or olive oil; freeze in ice cube trays. Remove from the trays and store in plastic bags in your freezer through the long winter months. Each cube is the approximate equivalent of 2-1/2 to 3 tablespoons of basil. No, the flavor's not quite the same as fresh, but it certainly is better than dried basil, or none at all.

Starters

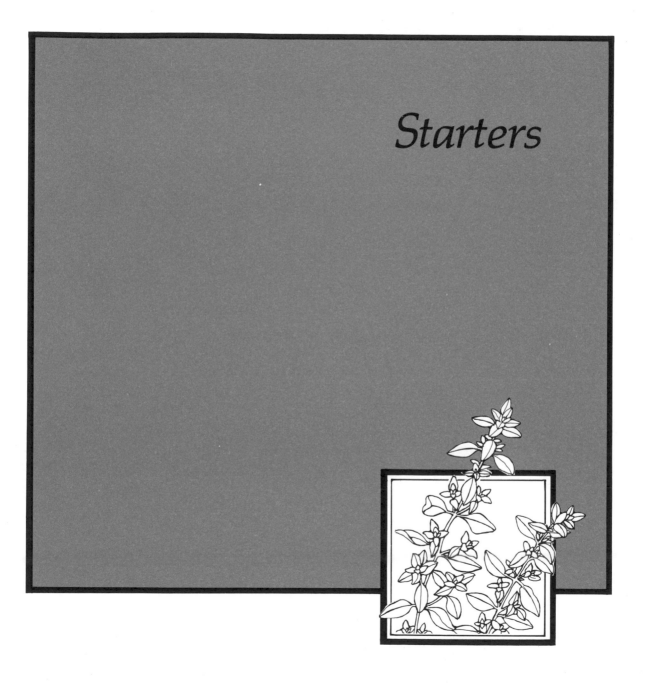

Using solely fresh ingredients to develop foods of culinary excellence has finally become a legitimate ideal in American restaurants. In the 1970s the thought of cooking with goat cheese was considered laughable, but that has fortunately changed.

The advent of an indigenous source of goat cheese allows restaurants greater latitude to provide new and exciting food products.

I wholeheartedly support the trend to use local foods, and I hope that this trend will promote styles of cooking that recognize goat cheese as good gastronomy.

Jonathan Waxman

CHÈVRE CROUTONS

From Cindy Pawlcyn, chef/owner of five restaurants, including Mustards and Fog City Diner, come these little coin-shaped croutons. They are outstanding served in a tossed salad, sprinkled on a soup or used as crackers with a dip or spread.

In a bowl or processor, combine into a smooth dough:

2/3 cup flour
3 tablespoons butter
5 ounces chèvre (chabis), crumbled

Roll the mixture into logs about as thick as a quarter coin. Chill, wrapped in wax paper, for at least one hour. Cut the logs into coin shapes about 1/4 inch thick. Prick with a fork and brush with:

1 egg white, lightly beaten

Sprinkle lightly with:

coarse sea salt

Bake for 15-20 minutes in a 375° oven until lightly browned. Cool and serve.

SMOKED SALMON PATÉ

Serves 6

Here is a fast, easy and popular appetizer to serve with crackers, French bread or fresh raw vegetables. It is especially easy to make if you have a food processor, though you must take some care if you use one. Fromage blanc turns to liquid if processed too much. It must be whipped quickly with the pulse button. Since fromage blanc is very mild, use mild salmon or lox to avoid overpowering the cheese flavor. The final result should be a white spread with salmon flecks. To achieve this, mix the salmon quickly but not thoroughly. Close attention to this is well worth the effort.

In a processor, or by hand, whip:

> **1-1/2 cups fromage blanc**
> **1 tablespoon chives, chopped**
> **3 cloves garlic, minced**

Mix lightly. Add:

> **4 ounces flaked mild smoked salmon or lox**
> **dash of cayenne pepper**

Blend until mixed, leaving flecks of salmon.

Serve chilled. This will keep for several days in the refrigerator, but it is usually consumed long before that.

LIPTAUER CHÈVRE

Serves 8-10

Mix thoroughly by hand, or in a processor:

8 ounces fresh chèvre (chabis or pyramide, rind removed)
4 ounces softened unsalted butter
1-1/2 tablespoons fresh chives, snipped fine
2 teaspoons anchovy paste
1 teaspoon capers, minced
1 teaspoon sharp mustard
1/2 teaspoon caraway seeds
1/2 teaspoon hot Hungarian paprika

Mound in a bowl. Garnish with:

1 teaspoon parsley, finely chopped
2 teaspoons black olives, minced
1/4 teaspoon paprika

Cover and chill thoroughly, up to 12 hours. Serve with thinly sliced pumpernickle or dark bread, and beer.

Note: 4 ounces fromage blanc in place of 4 ounces of chabis or pyramide makes this dip more tangy and soft.

BAKED CABECOU TOASTS

Serves 6

Titillate your senses with the uniquely rich and nutty flavor of toasted cabecou. These toasts are easy to handle, so they are perfect for hors d'oeuvres or snacks.

Lightly toast:
>**6 thin slices French bread baguette (preferably not sour dough)**

Spread sparingly on each slice of toast:
>**unsalted butter**

Carefully cut in half, preserving round shape:
>**3 cabecou, available preserved in olive oil**

Place cheese slices on prepared toasts on a cookie sheet and broil for 2-3 minutes, until cheese begins to brown and soften. They are best eaten warm.

OUR SOPHIE'S CHOICE

Serves 6

Sophie is an old family friend from Russia, who passed along this delightful baked cheese appetizer.

Mix together thoroughly:
> **5 ounces herb or pepper coated chèvre**
> **5 ounces plain chèvre (chabis)**
> **1 egg, beaten**
> **1/4 cup flour**

When mixed, form the mixture into a log shape about 2 inches in diameter. Roll it in:
> **approximately 1/4 cup flour or enough to make it somewhat stiff**

Place on a buttered cookie sheet. Before baking, brush with:
> **1 tablespoon melted butter**

Bake at 400° for 30 minutes, or until golden. Slice and serve warm.

BAKED CHÈVRE WITH WATERCRESS AND SPINACH

Serves 6

We were inspired here by Diane Worthington, author of *The Cuisine of California*, published by J.P. Tarcher, Inc. This is our version of her original concept. The contrast of colors, textures and tastes is dramatic. We especially recommend it as a first course, accompanied by a rich chardonnay.

Spoon into a small bowl:
> **4 tablespoons olive oil**

Spoon into another small bowl:
> **1/2 cup fine bread crumbs**

Soak in olive oil to thoroughly coat, then roll in bread crumbs to cover thickly:
> **2 5-ounce chabis, sliced crosswise in thirds**

Place on cookie sheet and refrigerate 1 hour.

Mix by hand or in blender until smooth, about 30 seconds:
> **1 cup olive oil**
> **1/3 cup sherry vinegar**
> **2 cloves garlic, finely chopped**
> **1 tablespoon Dijon mustard**
> **1/2 teaspoon salt**
> **Freshly ground pepper to taste**

Wash thoroughly and pat dry:
> **1 small bunch spinach**
> **1 bunch watercress, thick ends of stems removed**

Slice the greens into thin threads. Toss together with vinaigrette until thoroughly coated.

Bake breaded chèvre slices in 400° oven until brown, warm, and beginning to soften, approximately 5 to 10 minutes. Meanwhile, cover six salad plates with the greens. Place the baked cheese in the middle and evenly divide the following garnish:

6 sun-dried tomatoes, thinly sliced
　or
1 sweet red pepper, finely diced

GOAT IN A COAT

Serves 6-8

Created as an appetizer by San Francisco food stylist Scottie McKinney, this is substantial enough to serve 2-4 people as a light lunch. We recommend accompanying it with red wine or beer.

In a processor or by hand, mix until pastry forms a ball:
> **1-1/4 cups unsifted flour**
> **1/2 cup butter**
> **5 ounces chèvre (chabis)**

Refrigerate to chill, then roll out to 1/8 inch thick.

Place in the center of the circle of crust:
> **1 whole 5-ounce chèvre, coated with herbs, pepper, dill, or paprika**

Pull up pastry edges to enclose the cheese. Moisten edges with water and seal tightly. Place on baking sheet with folded edges down. Brush with:
> **1 egg, beaten**

Bake at 375° for 25-30 minutes, until golden.

To serve, surround with mounds of chopped tomatoes, scallions and Black Forest Ham. Accompany with dark bread.

CRAB FILLED TOMATOES

Serves 6

Start almost any meal with this cool and attractive offering.

Slice off tops, scoop out pulp, salt and invert for 15 minutes:
  6 medium tomatoes

Brush inside and out with the following marinade:
  1/2 cup oil
  3 tablespoons lemon juice
  1/2 teaspoon shallot, finely minced
  1/2 teaspoon Dijon mustard
  Salt and pepper to taste

Cut in half lengthwise, then in quarters crosswise, then in spears:
  1 small avocado

Soak avocado spears in remaining marinade.

Separate into firm sections:
  1/4 pound crab meat

Soak crab pieces in marinade with avocado.

Pack down lightly in bottom third of each tomato:
  3/4 cup fromage blanc with herbs (approximately 2 tablespoons each tomato)

Arrange avocado spears and crab pieces alternately, securing them in the fromage blanc.

SWEET ONION TARTS

Serves 4

These individual tarts are a fast, easy and impressive first course.

If you would like more bite-sized appetizers, cut the dough with a 2-inch cookie cutter and you will have 15-20 canapés. A full-bodied white wine, or light red wine, is a fine complement to these tender morsels.

Frozen puff pastry is available in most supermarkets. Make your own or defrost:
one sheet frozen puff pastry

Roll out the sheet to about 1-1/2 times its original size. Cut 4 rounds, approximately 6 inches in diameter. Place on a lightly oiled cookie sheet. Pierce several times with a fork. Bake for 15-20 minutes at 400°.

Peel, slice 1/4 inch thick, then coarsely chop:
1 large or 2 small red onions

Melt in large skillet:
2 tablespoons butter

Add the chopped onions and sauté until slightly tender. Mix in:
1/2 teaspoon salt
1/4 teaspoon pepper
1/2 teaspoon fresh thyme or 1/4 teaspoon dried

Divide onion mixture between the 4 prebaked tart shells. Top each tart with one quarter of:
8 ounces chèvre (pyramide or taupinière), crumbled

Place the tarts under the broiler for approximately 2-3 minutes until cheese begins to soften and brown slightly. Watch carefully. It is very easy to overcook at this point. Serve hot.

BEUREG

Serves 8-10

This is our adaptation of a savory Middle Eastern treat made with filo dough. These rice paper-thin sheets of dough are sold either fresh or frozen in 1 pound packages.

Keep under a moist towel while working:

1 pound filo dough sheets, cut in half lengthwise

Melt:

1 cup butter

Remove from under towel up to 4 half sheets at a time. Brush each with butter, then fold over lengthwise. Brush top surface lightly with butter. Place one heaping teaspoon of filling (see below) on top corner. If you fill these too full, they will leak. Fold portion with filling over so you have a diagonal fold. Continue folding, like a flag, down the sheet, brushing lightly with butter after each fold. You will end up with a tight little triangle package, buttered on top, and ready to bake. Continue with remaining filo and filling. When all are ready, bake in 400° oven for 12-15 minutes until puffed and golden.

For filling, mix in processor, or by hand, in medium bowl:

8 ounces chèvre (pyramide)
2 eggs
1 tablespoon parsley, chopped
1 tablespoon fresh basil, chives or thyme, chopped
dash of salt and pepper
2 tablespoons fromage blanc,
    or
2 tablespoons cream, fresh or sour

CHÈVRE OLE!

Serves 4-6

This piquant south-of-the-border fare is fast and fun.

Pour into a medium bowl:
> **3/4 cup of your favorite salsa**

Add:
> **2 tablespoons fresh cilantro, chopped**
> **2 tablespoons olives, chopped**

Coat generously with the salsa:
> **4 flour or 6 corn tortillas**

Divide evenly and top the tortillas with:
> **5 ounces chèvre, thinly sliced**
> **4 ounces grated cheddar or jack cheese**

Place on cookie sheet in 350° oven, or under broiler. If baked, they will be ready in 5 minutes; if broiled, in 2 minutes. Serve immediately after cutting into wedges.

SCOTTIE'S SOUP

Serves 2

This simple soup, created by Scottie McKinney, is just as wonderful chilled as it is hot.

Melt in a medium saucepan:

2 tablespoons butter

Add:

1/2 cup shallots (approximately 4 large), finely chopped

Sauté shallots in butter until soft, but not browned.

Add:

2 cups chicken or vegetable stock

Heat until just below a simmer and then add, stirring steadily:

8 ounces chèvre (pyramide with ash rind removed), crumbled

Heat soup over low flame, stirring with a whisk until the cheese is melted and incorporated into the stock. Do not cook too long; 5 minutes is about right.

Serve immediately. It may be reheated, but be careful not to let it boil.

To serve, top with:

snipped chives and freshly ground pepper

CINDY'S SOUP

Serves 6

A rich and colorful beginning to a light meal, this soup is a definite winner. Many thanks to Cynthia Pawlcyn for creating and sharing this recipe.

Melt in 2-quart saucepan:
> **1/2 cup butter**

Add:
> **1/2 medium onion, minced**
> **1 medium carrot, grated**

Sauté until soft.

Add:
> **1 teaspoon dry mustard**
> **3/4 teaspoon sweet paprika**

Whisk in:
> **6 cups chicken or vegetable stock**

Simmer for 20 minutes, stirring every few minutes. Then add:
> **5 ounces chèvre (chabis), crumbled into small pieces**
> **4 ounces taupinière, rind removed, crumbled into small pieces**
> **1/4 cup freshly grated Parmesan**

Stir constantly for about 2 minutes, until cheese is thoroughly melted and incorporated.

First combine to a smooth paste, then add to stock mixture:
> **2 tablespoons cornstarch**
> **1/2 cup cream**

Beating constantly with a whisk, heat the soup until slightly thickened. Do not let boil or let the cheese scorch on the bottom.

Add:

Salt and pepper to taste

Serve with minced chervil or parsley sprinkled on top, or with the goat cheese croutons on page 23.

PARTY ROUNDS

Serves 12-16

A lively, lusty appetizer, this is sufficiently robust to serve with cocktails or red wine.

Sauté in a large skillet:

> **1 pound mild fresh sausage (pork or turkey)**
> **2 cloves garlic, minced or pressed**
> **1-2 small dried hot peppers, ground**
> > **or**
> **1-2 teaspoons red pepper flakes**
> **1 teaspoon ground cumin**

When sausage is lightly browned and crumbled, drain on several layers of paper toweling to remove much of the fat. When sausage mixture is cooled and well drained, mix with:

> **8 ounces chèvre (pyramide or taupinière), crumbled**
> **1 teaspoon fresh thyme or 1/2 teaspoon dried**

Have ready:

> **2 packages of cocktail rye bread rounds (8 ounce package)**
> > **or**
> **thinly sliced long baguette (20-24 inches)**

On a cookie sheet, lay out bread slices and evenly distribute some sausage/cheese mixture on each one. Rounds may be set aside at this stage for up to one hour.

When ready to serve, heat under the broiler for 3-4 minutes until hot. Watch carefully. Serve hot.

GOAT GOUGERE

Serves 4

Here is our adaptation of a French standard often served with red wine. One of the remarks from hungry taste testers was, "Hmmm, wouldn't I love a couple of these for breakfast!" So, feel free to serve goat gougere whenever you fancy.

Heat in a heavy medium saucepan over medium heat, stirring until mixture boils:

1 cup water
1/2 cup unsalted butter, cut into pieces
1/2 teaspoon salt
dash of freshly ground pepper

Add all at once:

1 cup flour

Beat for about one minute until mixture begins to form a ball. Remove from heat and let cool. This next step is very easy in a processor. Add to the mixture:

4 eggs, at room temperature

Beat until smooth and satiny after each addition.

Add:

5 ounces chèvre, fresh or aged (chabis, taupinière, crottin, calistogan, herb, or pepper)

Stir until well blended. Drop the paste by heaping tablespoons onto a large buttered and floured baking sheet. Form into a circular, wreath shape. Bake in a 375° oven until well browned, about 35 minutes. Serve immediately, or while still warm.

SOME MORE IDEAS . . .

Place a whole or split 5-ounce chèvre on a serving plate. Pour about 3/4 cup of peach, mango or apple chutney over the cheese. Serve with crackers or toast rounds.

Arrange whole or sliced plain chèvre on a serving plate. Sprinkle the cheese with fresh or dried herbs of your choice and drizzle with olive oil or viniagrette. Serve with crackers, French bread or vegetable cruidités.

Place two whole or split 5-ounce chèvre rounds in a pint jar. Add to the jar: garlic cloves, parsley, a few peppercorns, a sprig of thyme and 1/2 of a bay leaf. Cover all with a virgin olive oil and let sit for a few days. Serve with your choice of crackers, bread or vegetables.

Split a pepper or herb cheese. Rub olive oil on the split side and place on a hot barbeque grill for about 30 seconds. Remove and serve immediately.

Spread sour rye bread with tapenade and goat cheese.

Roll goat cheese in a thin slice of prosciutto or Westphalian ham, heat in the oven until just warm and serve with a mustard or onion sauce.

Melt cheese on potato pancakes and serve with sautéed apples or homemade applesauce.

Serve a very fresh plain cheese with caviar and thinly sliced French bread (preferably not sourdough).

Mix cheese with garlic, capers or herbs and stuff into cherry tomato halves.

Combine cheese with herbs, garlic, chili peppers, bread crumbs, etc., and stuff mushroom caps. Serve cold or heated.

Serve chèvre mayonnaise (see recipe page 61) with raw oysters.

Fill puff pastry or filo with cheese, mushrooms, anchovies, herbs, sun-dried tomatoes, etc.; make bite-size packets and bake. This is a good use for leftover pastry or filo.

Stuff won ton skins with cheese, sautéed shitaki mushrooms, ginger, and deep fry.

Add extra garlic to the creamed spinach on page 82 and serve cold as a dip for fresh vegetables, crackers or bread.

Main Courses

My fascination for goat cheese continues to develop as new cheeses become available. The addition of goat cheese to a dish strengthens it. Goat cheese provides depths of flavor and aroma, adding an earthy, pungent dimension. At Spago we use goat cheese in pasta, pizza, salad and with lamb as a main course.

Wolfgang Puck

HOT SAUSAGES WITH FETTUCCINI

Serves 4-6

Our editor, Dorothy Foster Sly, suggested this hearty, fool-proof dish. Serve with a garden salad, French bread and a full-bodied zinfandel.

In a large skillet, brown over medium-high heat about 5 minutes:

    8 hot Italian sausages (approximately 1-1/2 pounds), cut into 1 inch pieces

When well browned, add:

    6 cloves garlic, finely minced
    1/2 cup fresh basil, finely chopped, or 1/4 cup prepared pesto
    6 tomatoes, peeled, seeded and quartered
    1/2 cup Marsala or red wine

Simmer over medium heat for 8-10 minutes until sauce is reduced slightly. While sauce is simmering, cook in boiling water:

    1 pound fresh fettuccini

Drain pasta and place in a large serving bowl or platter. Crumble over the hot pasta:

    5 ounces chèvre (chabis)

Add the sauce and toss together lightly.

Serve hot and offer:

    freshly grated Parmesan (optional)

GOAT CHEESE FILLING FOR PASTA

Serves 4

Here we present a mouth-watering filling for ravioli, manicotti shells or canneloni crêpes. For detailed instructions on making pasta, refer to a good basic Italian cookbook, such as *Classic Italian Cookery* by Marcella Hazan.

All the steps can easily be accomplished in a food processor.

Finely chop:
>**1 tablespoon parsley**
>**1 tablespoon fresh basil**
>**1 large shallot**

Add:
>**1/2 cup drained fromage blanc**
>**8 ounces chèvre (taupinière, pyramide, calistogan, or combination)**
>**1 egg**
>**1/2 teaspoon salt**
>**pinch of cayenne**
>**pinch of nutmeg**

Mix until smooth, then fill your chosen pasta. Cook; then serve with a pesto or marinara sauce, or try the following garlic cream sauce:

Melt in small saucepan:
>**3 tablespoons butter**

Add:
>**2 cloves garlic, minced**

Cook 1-2 minutes.

Then add:
>**3/4 cup cream**

Cook over medium heat until slightly thickened, approximately 5 minutes. Toss with or pour over your pasta. Sprinkle with:

1/2 cup grated fresh Parmesan cheese
2 tablespoons finely chopped parsley, chives or chervil

CALZONE

Serves 4

Its aroma stimulates. Its unique shape intrigues. Its complex flavors satisfy. Of Italian origin, this golden, crusty pizza-sandwich makes a delectable casing for a variety of savory goat cheese fillings (see following recipes).

To prepare the dough, dissolve:

1 envelope or 1 tablespoon yeast

In:

1-1/3 cups warm water

Add and mix together:

4 cups unbleached white flour
2 tablespoons olive oil
1 teaspoon salt

This is just the right amount of dough to prepare in a food processor, so if you have one, mix all the ingredients in the bowl using the steel blade and then run the machine for about one minute. Otherwise, mix the ingredients in a bowl and then knead for about 10 minutes or until shiny and elastic. (We use the processor and then remove the dough and knead by hand for 3-4 minutes until nice and elastic.) Place the dough in an oiled bowl, turn to coat with oil, cover the bowl with a towel and let rise about 1-1/2 hours or until double in bulk.

This amount of dough will make 2 large or 4 individual calzones. Divide the dough into the desired number and roll out to round shapes about 1/4 inch thick (18 inch diameter for large, 12 inch diameter for small). Paint lightly with olive oil, top with your desired filling on one half of the dough, leaving 1/2 inch border. Brush edges of dough with water. Fold the other half over, pressing edges together with fingers to seal, and flute. You should have a tight half circle package. Lightly brush the top with oil, cut two small slashes on top for steam vents, and place on a baking surface lightly sprinkled with corn meal. Bake in a very hot oven (450°) for 25-30 minutes for the large and 15-20 minutes for the small. Crust will be browned and puffed up. Ceramic baking stones are available for baking pizza and work well, but we were happy with the results from a cookie sheet.

All the following fillings are sufficient for two large or four small calzones. Instructions are given for preparing the two large ones, so adjust if you are making four.

CALZONE WITH SPINACH AND THREE CHEESES

Wash thoroughly:

1 pound spinach

Chop. Steam the spinach until limp. Drain thoroughly. Brush the prepared dough with olive oil and spread the spinach over one half of the dough. Sprinkle the spinach with these ingredients:

1 cup grated jack or Mozzarella cheese
10 ounces chèvre (chabis), crumbled
4 cloves garlic, finely minced
1 tablespoon dried oregano
1/4 teaspoon cayenne pepper
2 tablespoons capers
1/4 cup freshly grated Parmesan

Fold, oil and bake. (See preceding instructions.)

CALZONE WITH CHANTERELLES

This is for those lucky enough to live where the rare chanterelle mushrooms grow wild, or where a specialty food market offers them. The rest of us can only dream.

In a medium skillet, melt:

2 tablespoons unsalted butter

Add and sauté for 3-4 minutes:

1 cup sliced fresh chanterelles
1 clove garlic, minced

Arrange the sauteed chanterelles on the dough and then cover with the following ingredients:

8 ounces chèvre (pyramide), crumbled
8 ounces jack or Mozzarella cheese, grated
2 tablespoons fresh parsley, chopped
1 tablespoon fresh marjoram, minced

Fold, oil and bake. (See preceding instructions.)

CALZONE WITH FRESH VEGETABLES

Melt in a 12-inch skillet:

2 tablespoons butter

Add and sauté for 5-8 minutes:

1 red pepper, thinly sliced
1 green pepper, thinly sliced
1/2 large white onion, chopped medium

Remove skillet from heat and add:

4 cloves garlic, chopped
1/4 pound fresh mushrooms, thinly sliced
1 teaspoon fresh rosemary or 1/2 teaspoon dried
1 tablespoon fresh oregano or 1 teaspoon dried
1/2 teaspoon fresh thyme or 1/4 teaspoon dried
2 small tomatoes, seeded, drained and chopped roughly

Spread above mixture evenly on one half of each round of rolled out dough. Top with the following ingredients, dividing evenly between the two calzones:

2 tablespoons olive oil, drizzled
4 ounces chèvre (goat fourme or taupinière), sliced
3 ounces Mozzarella, grated
3-4 tablespoons, freshly grated Parmesan

Fold, oil and bake. (See preceding instructions.)

CALZONE WITH GARLIC AND PROSCIUTTO

Seed, peel and thickly slice:
> **4 fresh tomatoes**

Arrange the tomato slices on half the dough. Sprinkle with the following:
> **1/4 pound prosciutto, thinly sliced and chopped**
> **8 ounces chèvre (pyramide or taupinière), crumbled**
> **1 tablespoon fresh thyme or 1 teaspoon dried**
> **4-6 cloves garlic, finely minced or pressed**
> **1/4 cup parsley, finely chopped**
> **8 ounces jack or Mozzarella cheese, grated**

Fold, oil and bake. (See preceding instructions.)

FUSILLI SEBASTOPOL

Serves 4

The origin of this fun-to-eat pasta dish is the small town of Sebastopol, California. Corkscrew shaped fusilli pasta is the perfect vehicle for this luscious chèvre sauce.

In a 10- or 12-inch skillet, heat:
>   **2 tablespoons olive oil**

Add:
>   **2 large cloves garlic, minced or pressed**
>   **4 ounces prosciutto, (aged Italian ham) finely chopped**
>   **1/2 cup sliced black or green ripe olives**

Sauté until garlic is soft, 3-5 minutes. Add:
>   **1 cup heavy cream**
>   **1 tablespoon fresh basil, finely chopped**
>   **1 teaspoon dried oregano or 1 tablespoon fresh**
>   **3 tomatoes, peeled, seeded and chopped**

Cook over medium heat until sauce is slightly thickened, 5-8 minutes. Add to sauce:
>   **4-5 ounces chèvre, crumbled**

Warm until cheese is just melted and sauce is smooth. In a large pan of boiling water, cook al dente (until soft but still springy):
>   **3/4 pound fusilli noodles**

Drain noodles and toss with the cheese sauce. Serve hot and offer:
>   **freshly grated Parmesan cheese**

PLUMPED POUSSIN

Serves 1

The strong, clean and rich flavors of this dish go well with steamed and buttered green beans or asparagus and wild rice. Accompany with a light red or full-bodied white wine.

For each person, you will need:
> **1 poussin (small young chicken) or 1 game hen**

With breast side up, carefully slip your fingers between the skin and breast meat on each side of the breast bone. For each bird you are preparing, make a mixture consisting of:
> **1 clove garlic, finely minced or pressed**
> **1 teaspoon lemon juice**
> **1 tablespoon olive oil**
> **1/2 teaspoon fresh thyme, rosemary or parsley (any fresh herb will do)**
> **1/8 teaspoon each, salt and pepper**

Sprinkle cavity with above mixture and also put a little in the small pockets under the skin on each side of breast bone. Then insert under the skin on each side of breast:
> **Approximately 1/2 ounce chèvre**

Rub skin with a little olive oil or butter and then place on a rack in a baking pan. Bake for one hour at 375°, basting with pan juices every 15 minutes. Serve hot.

Serves 4

These boneless chicken breast pastries are beautiful and actually quite simple to prepare if you use frozen puff pastry.

Skin and bone:

4 chicken half-breasts (6-8 ounces each)

In a small bowl, mix with a fork or back of a spoon:

5 ounces chèvre (chabis)
1 large clove garlic, minced or pressed
1 tablespoon fresh thyme
 or
2 tablespoons fresh basil, chopped
 or
2 tablespoons fresh chives, chopped

Make your own puff pastry or defrost:

1 package (17.5 ounces) frozen puff pastry

Unfold both pieces of pastry and roll one sheet out into a rectangle about 1/8 inch thick. Cut in half. Repeat with the second sheet. You will have four rectangles, each approximately 7 x 10 inches.

Spread one quarter of the cheese mixture in the approximate shape of a chicken breast on the middle of each pastry sheet, lengthwise. Sprinkle cheese with salt and pepper. Place chicken breasts on top of the cheese. Depending upon the size and shape of the chicken breasts, you may have to trim away some of the pastry. To ensure a proper seal, the pastry should extend 1 inch beyond the chicken breast on the long ends. Lift the short ends of the pastry to meet in the center. Pinch together. Press and flute the long ends, enclosing the chicken in a tight envelope. Brush with:

1 beaten egg

Place envelopes, seam side down, on a baking sheet. Bake in 425° oven until pastry is browned, about 25 minutes.

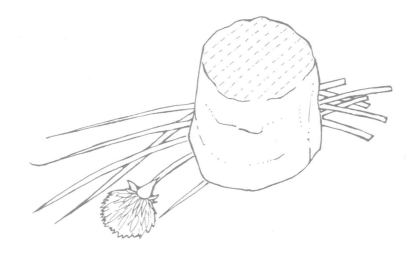

MT. OLYMPUS PIE

Serves 10

Goats were important in Greek mythology. Dionysius and Zeus were said to have been nurtured by female goats and raised on their milk. Cloven-hoofed Pan was the god of flocks. We've named this heavenly version of a Greek spinach pie after the home and playground of these gods.

Place in a small bowl:

1/4 cup raisins

Pour boiling water on raisins to cover. Let sit for 15 minutes to plump.

In a small skillet, place:

1/4 cup pine nuts

Dry-roast pine nuts over medium flame. Shake the pan regularly and roast the nuts until just starting to brown. Cool and reserve.

Wash, dry and roughly chop:

2 bunches spinach (approximately 2 pounds)

In a large skillet, melt:

2 tablespoons butter

Add:

1 medium onion, chopped

Sauté until soft and just beginning to brown. Add the readied spinach and heat until just wilted. Add the drained raisins and the roasted pine nuts and:

juice of 1/2 a lemon
salt and pepper to taste
6 eggs, lightly beaten
8-10 ounces chèvre (pyramide or taupinière or chabis), crumbled

Butter a 9 x 13-inch baking pan. Stir together:

1 cup melted butter

1/2 cup olive oil

Have ready:

1/2 pound filo dough

Line the baking pan with 5 sheets of the filo, brushing each sheet with the butter/olive oil combination as you lay them out. Spread the spinach mixture over the five sheets of dough. Top with the remaining sheets of filo, brushing each again with the butter and oil. Brush the top sheet and bake at 350° for 45 minutes. Cool 15 minutes before cutting into squares.

EGGPLANT CHÈVRE

Serves 4

This concoction received countless "oohs" and "ahhhs" when it was first served at our annual grape crush and wine making party. What a perfect accompaniment to a full-bodied California Zinfandel.

Slice 1/2 inch thick:
> **one large or 2 small eggplants (about 1-1/2 pounds)**

Salt eggplant slices lightly on both sides and place in a colander to sweat. After about 20 minutes, pat dry each slice. Brush each slice on both sides with:
> **olive oil**

Place slices on a cookie sheet and then under the broiler. Broil on each side until browned, watching carefully so as not to burn. When both sides are browned, remove from cookie sheet and arrange in a 9 x 13-inch baking pan.

Remove skin and seeds from:
> **5 medium tomatoes**

Slice the tomatoes about 1/2-inch thick and arrange them on top of the eggplant slices.

Mix together:
> **1/4 cup fresh basil, chopped**
> **4-5 cloves garlic, minced**
> **1 teaspoon fresh thyme, chopped, or 1/2 teaspoon dried**
> **1 tablespoon fresh oregano, chopped, or 1 teaspoon dried**
> **2 tablespoons fresh parsley, chopped**

Sprinkle herb and garlic mixture over tomatoes and eggplant.

Cover with:
> **8 ounces chèvre (pyramide), crumbled**

Finally, sprinkle over casserole:
> **1/2 pound Mozzarella or jack cheese, grated**

Bake in a 350° oven for 30 minutes. Let cool 10 minutes before serving.

GRILLED FISH WITH CHÈVRE MAYONNAISE

Serves 4

This mayonnaise is quite versatile. It is delicious as a sauce for any fresh, firm-fleshed, grilled fish. Especially recommended are tuna, salmon or sturgeon. It is also a great dip for artichokes and tasty with other vegetables, potatoes and bread.

Prepare the mayonnaise in a blender or processor. Blend together at low speed:

> **1 egg yolk**
> **1/4 cup oil**
> **1 cup fromage blanc, with or without herbs**

When thickened, add:

> **1 teaspoon hot mustard**
> **1 teaspoon lemon juice**
> **1 clove garlic (if using fromage blanc without herbs)**
> **salt and pepper to taste**
> **small quantities of fresh herbs to taste**

Blend until completely combined, approximately 5-10 seconds.

Build a good hot fire on your charcoal grill. Butter or oil:

> **4 fish filets or steaks (6-8 ounces each)**

Place on the fire. Grill for about 3 minutes on each side. Be careful not to overcook the fish or it will crumble and fall into the fire, not to mention lose its beautiful flavor. Remove fish from grill and place a dollop of chèvre mayonnaise on top. Offer extra mayonnaise.

FISH FILET FLORENTINE

Serves 4

In a medium saucepan, melt:
>**1 tablespoon butter**

Add:
>**2 small shallots, finely minced**
>**1 tablespoon fresh basil, chopped or 1 teaspoon dried**
>**1 tablespoon fresh parsley, chopped**

Sauté until soft but not browned. Add:
>**1/2 cup heavy cream**

Simmer until slightly thickened, about 5 minutes. Add:
>**5 ounces chèvre (chabis), crumbled**

Stirring constantly, heat sauce on medium flame until cheese is just melted and sauce is smooth. Remove from heat and cover.

Wash well:
>**2 bunches fresh spinach (approximately 2 pounds)**

Coarsely chop spinach. Steam until just limp. Drain thoroughly.

In a small skillet, melt:
>**1 tablespoon butter**

Add and sauté 2 minutes:
>**1/2 cup chopped green onion**

Mix spinach and green onion and spread evenly over the bottom of a lightly buttered casserole dish. On the top of the spinach mixture, arrange:

4 lingcod filets or rock fish filets (approximately 1-1/2 pounds)

Sprinkle with:

1/4 teaspoon salt
1/4 teaspoon pepper

Dot fish filets with:

4 teaspoons butter

Cover and bake in 425° oven for 12-15 minutes, depending upon thickness of filets. When fish is springy to the touch but does not yet flake, remove from the oven and turn on the broiler. Pour the cheese sauce over the cooked fish. Place the casserole, uncovered, under the broiler for 2-3 minutes until sauce is bubbly and speckled with brown. Serve immediately.

OYSTERS HATHAWAY

Serves 4

Though we consider this to be a main course, it can easily be adapted as a starter to a light meal. In that case, serve 2-3 oysters per person. Champagne is the perfect accompaniment.

In a large skillet, melt:

> **2 tablespoons butter**

Add:

> **1/2 pound mushrooms, finely chopped**
> **2 shallots, finely chopped**
> **1/2 cup parsley, finely chopped**

Sauté until liquid is evaporated.

Add:

> **2 tablespoons brandy**

Cook mushroom mixture until brandy is absorbed. Mixture should be moist, but with no standing liquid. Set aside.

To prepare sauce, melt:

> **2 tablespoons butter**

Add:

> **2 tablespoons shallots, finely minced**

Sauté until translucent.

Add:

> **1/2 cup heavy cream**

Stir sauce over high heat for about five minutes to reduce.

Add:

> **1 tablespoon brandy**
> **3 ounces mild chèvre**

Cook, stirring until chèvre is just melted and sauce is smooth.

Season to taste with:

white pepper
salt

Set aside.

Shuck, saving the 16 deepest half shells:

16 oysters

Poach oysters as follows.

In a large skillet, melt:

2 tablespoons butter

Add:

1/2 cup vermouth

Place oysters and their liquor in the butter/vermouth mixture and simmer until firm, turning each oyster once.

Divide mushroom mixture evenly into oyster half-shells. Remove oysters from poaching liquid with a slotted spoon. Place one oyster over mushroom mixture on each half-shell. Pour approximately 1 tablespoon sauce on each oyster. Heat under the broiler for 2-3 minutes until bubbly and lightly browned. Watch carefully so they don't burn. Serve immediately.

For a very attractive service, place four oysters in the shell in individual ramekins on a bed of rock salt, one ramekin per serving.

PUCK'S RAMEKIN

Serves 4

Wolfgang Puck, chef/owner of the wildly popular Los Angeles restaurant, Spago, collaborated with one of his chefs, Dale Payne, to create this colorful dish for us.

Beat together:

> **1/2 cup cream**
> **3 eggs**
> **2 egg yolks**

Then mix in:

> **1/2 teaspoon fresh thyme or 1/4 teaspoon dried**
> **1/4 teaspoon ground coriander**
> **1/8 teaspoon cayenne**
> **1 teaspoon salt**
> **1/2 teaspoon freshly ground black pepper**

Clean thoroughly:

> **12 large swiss chard leaves**

Cut off the bottom white rib section and slice in fine julienne. Chop the leaves medium fine.

Melt in a large skillet:

> **3 tablespoons butter**

Add:

> **1 large shallot, finely minced**

Sauté 4-5 minutes over medium heat, until softened but not brown. Add the chopped chard leaves and stems and sauté until just wilted.

Crumble into pea-sized pieces:

> **2 5-ounce chèvres (chabis or plain disks).**

Reserve approximately 1/3 of the crumbled cheese.

Mix the remaining 2/3 crumbled cheese with the chard and the egg/cream mixture.

Generously butter:

4 (one cup size) ramekins or individual custard cups

Fill cups approximately 3/4 full with mixture, leaving room for expansion. Place cups over—not in—slowly simmering water on top of the stove. Cover and simmer gently for about 15-20 minutes, or until a small knife inserted in the center comes out clean.

Turn out upside down onto an oven-proof plate or baking pan. Top evenly with reserved crumbled cheese. Place under broiler for approximately 2 minutes, or until cheese has softened and is beginning to brown.

To serve, remove from baking pan and place each one in the center of a plate in a pool of tomato/basil vinaigrette. Top with a single perfect basil leaf.

Tomato/Basil Vinaigrette:

Peel, seed, then chop into 1/4 inch dice:

2 medium tomatoes

Mix together with:

4 large leaves fresh basil, finely minced
1 large shallot, finely minced
2 tablespoons olive oil
1 tablespoon vinegar
salt and pepper

STUFFED LAMB WITH HONEY GLAZE

Serves 8-10

Prepare stuffing mixture as follows.

Clean carefully and remove stems from:
> **1 bunch fresh spinach**

Steam the spinach in its own moisture until just wilted. Drain well. In a large skillet, heat:
> **1/4 cup olive oil**

Add and sauté:
> **1 medium onion or 6 green onions, finely chopped**
> **1/2 cup fresh parsley, chopped**
> **3 large cloves garlic, finely minced**
> **1/2 teaspoon dried oregano**
> **1/8 teaspoon cayenne pepper**

When onion and garlic are soft, chop the spinach and add to the herb/onion mixture. Sauté another 3 minutes. Cool the mixture and add:
> **1/2 cup fine bread crumbs**
> **1 egg, lightly beaten**

Have your butcher bone and butterfly:
> **5-6 pound leg of lamb**

Place it on a work surface fat side down, and flatten it as much as possible. Rub the surface with:
> **1 tablespoon olive oil**
> **2 teaspoons lemon juice**
> **a sprinkling of salt and pepper**

Spread the spinach mixture evenly over the lamb surface. Crumble over the spinach:

5 ounces chèvre (chabis, calistogan, or combination)

Carefully roll the lamb, enclosing the spinach mixture. Tie securely. Coat the top and sides of the rolled and tied roast with:

2 tablespoons honey

Place on a rack in a roasting pan in a 425° oven for 10 minutes. Lower the temperature to 375° and roast for 15-20 minutes per pound until medium rare. Remove from oven and let sit 15 minutes before carving and serving.

GOAT-CRUSTED PORK ROAST

Serves 6-8

This succulent and aromatic crusted roast provides a unique twist to an old standard. It is equally as sumptuous made with lamb.

Have at room temperature:
> **4-pound pork loin or well trimmed butt roast**

Mix together in a food processor or with a fork:
> **1 teaspoon fresh thyme, finely chopped, or 1/2 teaspoon dried**
> **1/2 teaspoon fresh rosemary, finely chopped, or 1/4 teaspoon dried**
> **4 cloves garlic, minced or pressed**
> **1-1/2 cups fresh bread crumbs**
> **5 ounces fresh chèvre, crumbled**
> **2 tablespoons olive oil**

The above mixture should be fairly moist so that it will stick together. For that reason use fresh bread crumbs (easy to make in a grinder or processor). If you must use dry bread crumbs, add a little water to moisten them.

Press the cheese mixture over the top and sides of the roast (but not the bottom) until you have a firm coating. Place in a roasting pan and cover. Roast at 325° for 30 minutes per pound or until meat thermometer reads 180°. To allow crust to brown slightly, remove cover 30 minutes before you expect roast to be done. When cooked, remove from oven and let sit 10-15 minutes before carving. If cooking the lamb roast variation, allow 20-25 minutes per pound for medium rare.

SOME MORE IDEAS . . .

Mix goat cheese with pine nut/rice stuffing for grape leaves.

Melt chèvre on top of hamburgers and steaks.

Use chèvre in enchiladas or, for a real treat, stuff in chili rellenos.

Use goat cheese in lasagne.

For a simple pasta sauce, mix chèvre with pesto.

Use our goat cheese filled ravioli on page 46 but serve in a flavorful chicken or vegetable broth and sprinkle with fresh herbs.

Mix fromage blanc with shallots, fresh herbs and pepper and serve over steak.

Use the spinach/chèvre stuffing for the leg of lamb on page 68 to stuff tomato halves or large mushroom caps instead.

Light Entrees & Accompaniments

Most cheeses fill you up, are too rich, tend to take over and leave no room for anything else. Goat cheese is not rich in a way that makes it impossible to combine with other things on a menu. It has a nice melting quality, too. Unlike other cheeses, it doesn't gum or congeal when it cools.

Alice Waters
Chez Panisse
Berkeley, California

GREEN BEAN SALAD

Serves 6-8

This was first tried in the heat of the summer, our gardens overflowing with green beans. If there is no such bounty for you, almost any type of fresh green beans prepared in this manner will provide a tasty accompaniment to simply grilled meats or fish.

Trim and cut in half lengthwise:
> **1-1/2 pounds green beans**

Steam until tender, approximately 5 minutes. Remove from steamer and immediately immerse in cold water to preserve color and texture.

In a large bowl, place:
> **1 medium red onion, coarsely chopped**
> **3/4 cup black Greek-style olives, pitted and quartered**

Add the cooled green beans.

Crumble and add:
> **8 ounces chèvre (pyramide), rind removed**

In a small bowl, mix until thoroughly blended:
> **3 tablespoons sherry vinegar**
> **7 tablespoons olive oil**
> **1-2 cloves garlic, pressed**
> **1/4 teaspoon cayenne pepper**
> **1/2 teaspoon salt**

Pour over the salad and toss gently. Try not to break up the pieces of cheese.

CHEZ PANISSE BAKED GOAT CHEESE WITH GARDEN SALAD

Serves 4

Alice Waters is the innovative chef/owner of Chez Panisse in Berkeley, California. She is renowned for, among other things, her use of goat cheese. Here is her "signature" salad.

Marinate for a day:

4 one-half-inch thick rounds of fresh goat cheese (approximately 8 ounces total)
3-4 sprigs fresh thyme

In:

1/4 cup virgin olive oil

Mix together:

1 cup fine dry bread crumbs
1 teaspoon dried thyme

Prepare a vinaigrette by whisking together:

1/2 cup virgin olive oil
2-3 tablespoons red wine vinegar
salt and pepper to taste

Wash and dry:

about 4 handfuls of garden lettuces (rocket, lamb's lettuce, small oak leaf and red leaf lettuces, chervil)

Slice into 24 slices about 1/4-inch thick:

a day old baguette

Melt:

about 1/2 cup butter

Brush each slice of baguette with some melted butter. Bake in a preheated 350° oven for 5-7 minutes, until the croutons are light golden brown.

Peel and cut in half:

2-3 cloves garlic

While still warm, rub each crouton with a cut clove of garlic.

Dip marinated cheese slices in the bread crumbs, and place on a lightly oiled baking dish. Bake in a preheated 400° oven for about 6 minutes, until cheese is lightly bubbling and golden brown. Toss the lettuces with enough vinaigrette to lightly coat and arrange them on 4 round salad plates. Place the cheese in the center of the plates with the more browned side up, and arrange the croutons around the cheese.

BROCCOLI WITH WALNUT-CHÈVRE SAUCE

Serves 6

This combination of walnuts, chèvre and fresh herbs enhances any in-season vegetable.

In a medium saucepan, melt:

2 tablespoons butter or walnut oil

Add and sauté:

1/2 cup coarsely chopped walnuts

When walnuts are lightly toasted, add to the saucepan:

5 ounces chèvre (chabis, pyramide, taupinière), crumbled
6 tablespoons heavy cream
1/4 cup fresh parsley, chopped
1/4 cup fresh chives, chopped
1 tablespoon fresh oregano, chopped or 1 teaspoon dried

Stir until thoroughly mixed and cheese is melted. Keep warm.

Wash and trim ends and cut into spears:

1 pound fresh broccoli

Steam broccoli approximately 5 minutes until fork-tender. Arrange broccoli spears on a serving plate. Pour walnut-chèvre sauce over the broccoli, and serve hot.

CHÈVRE WITH RED CABBAGE

Serves 4-6

The contrast of the tart vinegar, the sweet shallots and cabbage, and the creamy chèvre create a sensational taste. Offer as a dramatic accompaniment to meat or poultry.

Steam until soft:

1 head red cabbage, shredded or thinly sliced

Melt over low heat in large saucepan:

4 tablespoons butter

Add:

2 large shallots, finely chopped

Sauté until soft but not brown, approximately 5 minutes. Add steamed cabbage to softened shallots and cook for 3 to 5 minutes, stirring occasionally.

Stir in:

2 tablespoons sherry vinegar

Crumble on top:

5 ounces chèvre (chabis)

Cover and heat thoroughly over a low flame for approximately 3 minutes.

Uncover, stir gently, and serve immediately.

HOT TOMATOES

Serves 2

Tomatoes filled in this manner are lively companions to a quickly seared steak. However, this voluptuous preparation may deserve center stage. The ingredients can easily be doubled to serve as a main course. The robust flavors of the slowly cooked onions and mushrooms are enhanced by the zesty tang of the cheese.

Cut off tops, squeeze out seeds and pulp, salt and invert:

> **2 medium tomatoes**

In a 10-inch skillet, melt:

> **2 tablespoons butter**

Add:

> **1 medium onion, chopped**

Sauté over low flame until slightly brown, fairly dry, and practically caramelized, approximately 10 minutes.

Remove onions from skillet and reserve.

Repeat above procedure with:

> **2 tablespoons butter**
> **1/4 pound mushrooms, thinly sliced**

When mushrooms are caramelized, reserve two mushroom slices. Then mix in onions.

Add:

> **1/4 cup chopped parsley**
> **salt and pepper to taste**

Have ready:

> **2-3 ounces chèvre (taupinière or calistogan), thinly sliced**

Fill the drained tomatoes with alternating layers of mushroom/onion mixture and chèvre, approximately three layers of each.

Place one caramelized slice of mushroom atop each tomato and bake in 350° oven 10-15 minutes.

CHÈVRE CREAMED SPINACH

Serves 4-6

Our Hungarian friend Manci makes a wonderful creamed spinach. Of course, we added goat cheese to her recipe and loved it even more. It is very rich, so is best served with simply grilled meats or poultry. Try stuffing this into tomatoes. Its luxurious texture is highlighted by the tart acidity of the tomatoes.

Simmer in a medium saucepan:

>**1/2 cup water**
>**1 pound fresh spinach, washed and chopped**
> **or**
>**1 package frozen spinach**

When fresh spinach is wilted, or frozen spinach is just defrosted, remove from heat. Thoroughly drain in a colander, reserving spinach liquid. If necessary, add water to reserved liquid to make 3/4 cup.

In a medium saucepan, heat:

>**1 tablespoon salad or olive oil**
>**1 tablespoon butter**

Add:

>**2 tablespoons flour**

Over low heat, cook until the raw taste of flour is gone, about 3-5 minutes. Do not allow to brown. Add:

>**1 large clove garlic, pressed**

Stirring constantly, thin the flour mixture by slowly adding reserved spinach liquid. Then add chopped spinach. Cook over low heat for 5-10 minutes. Just before serving, add:

>**5 ounces chèvre, crumbled**
>**salt and pepper to taste**

Stir over heat until cheese is just melted and hot. Serve.

PEAKS PIKE POTATOES

Serves 6

Potatoes, garlic and goat cheese seem to have a natural affinity for each other. We experimented frequently with this combination of ingredients. For that reason, we've named this recipe after the location of our test kitchen.

Wash thoroughly:

2 pounds baking potatoes

Thinly slice and keep covered with cold water until the cheese sauce is made.

Make the following cheese sauce in a blender. Put all the ingredients in at once and blend until smooth and well mixed, about 1 minute.

4-6 cloves garlic
1 teaspoon fresh thyme
2 tablespoons fresh parsley
1 cup cream or 1 cup yogurt
1/2 cup milk
2 tablespoons butter
2 tablespoons flour
5 ounces chèvre (chabis)

Butter a 9 x 13-inch shallow baking dish. Drain the potatoes and dry in a tea towel. Arrange one-half of the potato slices in the baking dish. Spread one-half of the cheese mixture over the potatoes and lightly salt and pepper. Layer the rest of the potatoes over the cheese. Spread the remaining cheese over the potatoes. Again, lightly salt and pepper.

Bake in a 350° oven for 1-1/2 hours. The top will be browned.

VEGETABLES GENOVESE

Serves 4-8

Chèvre pesto is delicious with almost any vegetable or combination of vegetables. Use your imagination, your favorites, whatever is in your refrigerator or in your garden. As a main course, this amply serves four. As an accompaniment to a simply-cooked meat or fish, this is enough for six to eight.

In 2-quart saucepan, steam together 4-5 minutes:
> **1 cup carrots, sliced 1/4 inch thick**
> **1 cup green beans, in 1-1/2 inch lengths**
> **1 cup cauliflower, broken into flowerettes**

Immerse in ice water to preserve color and texture. Drain and set aside.

Melt in a large skillet over medium heat:
> **1/4 cup butter**

Add:
> **1 large onion, cut in half, then sliced 1/4 inch thick**

Sauté about 2 minutes, then add:
> **1 large red pepper, sliced lengthwise 1/4 inch thick (if unavailable, omit)**

Sauté 1 minute. Add:
> **1/4 pound mushrooms, sliced 1/4 inch thick**
> **2 small zucchini, sliced 1/4 inch thick**

Stirring, continue to sauté another 2 minutes. Add reserved steamed vegetables, mixing lightly. Lower heat and toss in:
> **1/4 teaspoon fresh rosemary or 1/8 teaspoon dried**
> **2 teaspoons fresh oregano or 1/2 teaspoon dried**
> **1/2 teaspoon fresh thyme or 1/4 teaspoon dried**
> **1/4 teaspoon each, salt and pepper**

Place evenly over surface:

5 ounces chèvre (chabis), sliced

Cover and heat over low flame about 1 or 2 minutes or until cheese has just softened. To serve, lightly mix into vegetables:

1/2 cup prepared pesto (Italian basil, garlic and cheese paste, sold frozen or canned).

A SUN-DRIED BAGUETTE

Serves 4

Indulge in a dream of sun-filled Mediterranean days with this gutsy open-faced sandwich. Serve it with lots of Greek or Niçoise olives and a chilled Beaujolais.

Cut in half lengthwise:
1 French bread baguette, usually 20-24 inches long

Brush cut sides evenly on both halves with:
enough virgin olive oil to lightly cover

Place in 350° oven and bake for 5 minutes or until just starting to crisp. Remove from oven and cut each half into four pieces. Evenly space on the pieces of toasted bread:
12 sun-dried tomatoes, thinly sliced lengthwise

Slice into 4 pieces each:
2 5-6 ounce chèvre (chabis), or slice into 2 pieces each: 4 calistogans

Top tomatoes with cheese slices and drizzle any remaining tomato oil over the cheese.

Broil 2-4 minutes or until cheese softens and begins to brown and melt.

BAKED CHARD

Serves 4-6

As an accompaniment, this rich vegetable dish is best served with poached fish or roast chicken. Equally appealing as a light or vegetarian main course, its companions on the plate might well be steamed baby carrots and new potatoes.

Remove the lower part of the coarse rib, wash thoroughly and roughly chop:
> **1 pound red or green chard**

Bring to a boil in a heavy saucepan:
> **1/2 cup lightly salted water**

Add chard and simmer until just wilted. Drain the leaves and gently press out the excess water.

In a food processor or blender, mix thoroughly, about 15 seconds:
> **1 egg**
> **1 cup milk**
> **1/3 cup melted butter**
> **dash of cayenne pepper**
> **1/2 cup toasted bread crumbs, preferably French bread**
> **1 teaspoon anchovy paste**
> **8 ounces chèvre (pyramide)**

Combine the drained chard with the cheese mixture and place in a one quart casserole. Sprinkle the top with:
> **1/4 cup toasted bread crumbs**

Bake uncovered in a 350° oven for 35-40 minutes. Serve hot.

GOAT CHEESE AND SHITAKE MUSHROOM SALAD

Serves 4

Chef Jonathan Waxman incorporates a wide array of ingredients to give us this sumptuous salad. His imaginative style is both complex and elegant.

Wash, dry and mix together:
>**4 heads small mixed lettuces**

Cut into thin strips:
>**2 whole red peppers, roasted, peeled and seeded**

Heat in a small skillet:
>**1 tablespoon olive oil**

Add:
>**1/4 pound whole fresh Shitake (large, meaty oriental mushrooms)**
>>**or**
>
>**2 ounces dried, soaked in hot water 30 minutes**

Sauté over medium heat until slightly softened, about 3 minutes.

Boil water in a medium saucepan and add:
>**1/4 pound asparagus, trimmed**
>**1/4 pound haricots verts (thin French green beans)**

Cook approximately 4 minutes or until still firm but not crunchy. Plunge immediately into ice water to preserve color.

Combine thoroughly:
>**1 shallot, chopped**
>**1/4 cup olive oil**
>**1 tablespoon Champagne vinegar**

Coat with oil and place on a cookie sheet:
5 ounces chèvre (chabis), sliced into quarters

Roast in 450° oven until softened, about 3 minutes.

Toss the lettuces with the vinaigrette and arrange the other ingredients attractively.

GOAT CHEESE SOUFFLÉ

Serves 4

This is an incredibly easy and very reliable version of a soufflé created at Le Petit Robert restaurant in New York.

Preheat oven to 450°.

Mix together thoroughly:
    3 egg yolks, beaten
    dash of salt and cayenne pepper
    2 ounces chèvre (taupinière or chabis)
    2 ounces (2 tablespoons) fromage blanc, with or without herbs

Beat in a separate bowl until stiff, but not quite dry:
    8 egg whites

Fold beaten whites carefully into cheese mixture. Pour into 4 individual, buttered soufflé dishes. Bake in the preheated oven 15-20 minutes or until fully risen and browned. Serve immediately.

For a delicious variation, add chopped, steamed fresh asparagus to the yolk mixture.

LEEK AND GOAT CHEESE TART

Serves 6

Leeks and goat cheese were made for each other. This tart is a fairly simple way to enjoy the combination. Serve either as a starter or for lunch or brunch. Excellent with a light white wine such as Gewurztraminer or a dry German Riesling.

Prepare your favorite flaky pastry dough and line a 10-inch tart pan.

In a medium skillet, melt:

4 tablespoons butter

Add and sauté gently for about 20 minutes:

6 medium leeks, washed and thinly sliced (white part only)

As the leeks cook and soften, add:

salt and pepper to taste
4-5 tablespoons water

Meanwhile, mix together thoroughly in a processor or by hand:

4 tablespoons butter, softened
8 ounces chèvre (pyramide)
2 eggs
1/2 cup cream
1/2 teaspoon fresh thyme or 1/4 teaspoon dried

Spread leeks on the prepared crust. Pour chèvre mixture evenly over them. Bake at 400° for approximately 30 minutes or until set and top is brown.

TART PROVENÇAL

Serves 6

This lively tart is suitably accompanied by a hearty red wine, perhaps a Zinfandel. Serve with a crisp green salad.

Prepare a crust of your choice and place in a removable bottom 10-inch tart pan.

Heat in a medium skillet:

> **2 tablespoons olive oil**

Add:

> **2 firm tomatoes, thickly sliced**
> **2 cloves garlic, chopped**

Sauté over medium heat for about 1 minute, turning tomatoes once. Place tomato slices and garlic on crust.

Cover tomatoes with:

> **5-6 ounces chèvre (chabis), sliced**
> **1 tablespoon fresh or 1 teaspoon dried oregano**
> **4-5 ounces grated Gruyère**

Mix together, then pour over tart:

> **2 eggs**
> **1/2 cup cream**
> **1/4 teaspoon salt**
> **1/8 teaspoon pepper, freshly ground**

Decorate with:

> **1/4 cup Niçoise or Greek olives, pits removed (or warn your guests!)**
> **and/or**
> **4 anchovy filets, chopped or whole**

Bake at 400° for about 1/2 hour or until puffed and slightly brown.

Cool to room temperature before serving.

CHESTNUT TART

Serves 6

This savory tart is excellent for brunch with a fruit salad. Or, as a first course, serve warm, cut in small slices. It is best to use fresh chestnuts for flavor, as well as texture. Canned chestnuts tend to be too soft, so if you must use them, dry them in a warm oven (300°) for about 20 minutes.

Line an 8-inch tart pan with your favorite crust. Weight and prebake for 15 minutes. Remove and cool while preparing the filling.

Cut a small "X" in the hard skin on the flat side of:

15-18 fresh chestnuts

Cover the chestnuts with water in a medium saucepan. Bring water to boil, then reduce heat and simmer for 25 minutes. Drain off boiling water and immerse chestnuts in cold water. Peel them while still warm, removing both hard shell and inner brown skin. Grind the chestnuts in a food processor or blender until the texture of cornmeal.

Mix together in a food processor or blender:

5 ounces fresh chèvre (chabis)
1/2 cup heavy cream
2 tablespoons unsalted butter
1/4 cup finely chopped onion
1/4 teaspoon salt
1/8 teaspoon pepper
2 eggs
2 tablespoons freshly grated Parmesan cheese

Blend the above ingredients until light and fluffy, about 30 seconds. Mix chestnuts into egg/cheese mixture until just combined. Then pour mixture into partially baked tart shell. Bake in 375° oven for 30-35 minutes or until solid and browned. Cool for at least 10 minutes before serving.

ASPARAGUS AND POACHED EGGS WITH TRIPLE-BLANCHED GARLIC SAUCE

Serves 4

This light, yet satisfying springtime brunch suggestion is especially wonderful with Champagne and good friends on a Sunday morning.

In each of three small pans, bring to a boil 1 to 2 cups water. Throw into the first pan for 30 seconds:

> **12 large cloves garlic, peeled**

Remove with a slotted spoon, then repeat procedure with the remaining two pans. Remove garlic from the third pan and add it to the following mixture in a small saucepan:

> **1 cup milk**
> **1 cup heavy cream**
> **10 ounces strong flavored chèvre (taupinière), broken up, rind removed**
> **dash of nutmeg**
> **salt and pepper to taste**

Stirring constantly, bring to a boil. Lower heat and simmer for about 20 minutes, continuing to stir frequently. By now it should be thickened. Remove from heat, cover to keep warm, and follow the next three steps.

Steam until tender, approximately 5 minutes:

> **1 pound asparagus, tough ends removed**

Poach to your liking:

> **4 eggs**

Toast and butter:

> **4 thick slices French bread, homemade bread, peasant bread, or English muffins**

Blend the garlic-cheese sauce in a blender until smooth, about 10-15 seconds. To assemble, spoon some of the sauce onto the center of a plate, then place a buttered piece of toast on the sauce. Next, place some steamed asparagus on top of the toast, top with a poached egg and spoon more sauce on top. Decorate plates with any extra asparagus. Serve immediately.

SUMMER OMELET

Serves 1

Summer brings us a profusion of vine-ripened tomatoes, aromatic basil and parsley, fresh goat cheese and eggs. We can never resist this natural combination. Serve this omelet for brunch, lunch or light supper, accompanied by warm bread and sliced tomatoes sprinkled with parsley.

Over medium heat, melt in a small skillet:
> **1/2 tablespoon butter**

Add:
> **1/2-1 small clove garlic, minced or pressed**
> **1 tablespoon fresh basil, chopped**

Stirring, cook about 1 minute. Remove from heat and set aside.

Beat together:
> **2 eggs**
> **1 tablespoon milk or water**
> **dash of salt and pepper**

Melt over medium heat in an 8- to 10-inch omelet pan or skillet:
> **1 tablespoon butter**

When bubbly, pour in the egg mixture and cook, lifting cooked bottom gently to allow uncooked portion to run underneath. Keep omelet from sticking to pan by gently shaking while it cooks. When eggs are beginning to set, but are still rather liquid on top, add the basil/garlic mixture and:
> **1-2 ounces chèvre (chabis or pyramide), crumbled**

Continue to cook, shaking pan gently and lifting omelet edges until it is no longer liquid, but still moist.

To serve, slide half the omelet onto a serving plate and fold the half that is still in the pan over onto the half that is on the plate.

For a variation, omit the basil and garlic and substitute 1/8 pound chopped smoked salmon and 2 teaspoons fresh or 1 teaspoon dried dill. Add to omelet with the goat cheese.

SOME MORE IDEAS . . .

Mash boiled potatoes with butter, salt, pepper and herbed fromage blanc. For a subtly intriguing flavor, include boiled celeriac (celery root).

Use fromage blanc, herbed or plain, on baked potatoes instead of sour cream. Or cut the baked potatoes in half and remove the potato pulp. Mix the pulp with butter, salt, pepper, chives and goat cheese. Return the mixture to the skins and reheat until the top is crispy.

Top an omelette with a dollop of herb fromage blanc.

Crumble cheese on fresh tomato slices or alternate tomato slices on a plate with sliced cold or warmed cheese. Sprinkle with herbs (basil, thyme, chives) virgin olive oil, salt and pepper.

Crumble cheese on top of tomato halves and heat under the broiler for a couple of minutes.

Use goat cheese in place of cream cheese with lox, bagels, red onion and tomato slices.

Add cheese to scrambled eggs just before they are set.

Add goat cheese to your favorite sweet or savory tarts and quiches.

Add crumbled goat cheese to the viniagrette recipe with the Green Bean Salad on page 75 and use for a salad dressing as you would a roquefort viniagrette.

For a delicious change of pace at breakfast, warm some goat cheese and offer with warmed honey or maple syrup, homemade bread, and pears or other in-season fruit.

Desserts

New channels of creativity were opened for me when I discovered Laura Chenel's Chèvre. Until then, I had never thought of using goat cheese in cooking. This domestic cheese compares with the French in a favorable way. The significant difference is that there is a sharp bitterness in most French Chèvres that isn't present in Laura Chenel's Chèvre.

Larry Forgione

DREAM COOKIES

About 2-1/2 dozen

These light cookies are always a hit. Though any type of preserves makes a good filling, apricot or berry are our favorites. They are most tasty still warm from the oven.

If you have a food processor, put all the ingredients in at once; process until smooth and the dough forms a ball. Otherwise, cream:

> **1/2 cup butter**
> **3 ounces mild chèvre (chabis)**

Mix in thoroughly:

> **1 cup flour**

Form into a ball, wrap in plastic and refrigerate at least one hour. Remove from refrigerator and roll out until thin, preferably using a pastry cloth and a covered rolling pin. Using a round cookie cutter or a drinking glass 2 to 2-1/2 inches in diameter, cut into individual rounds.

Place in the middle of each cookie round:

> **1/4 teaspoon apricot or raspberry preserves**
> **1/8 teaspoon mild chèvre (chabis)**

Moisten the edges, fold in half and lightly press edges together. You will have half moon cookie puffs. Sprinkle with:

> **white granulated sugar**

Place on a lightly greased cookie sheet. Bake at 375º for 15 minutes, or until just slightly browned.

GOAT CHEESE ICE CREAM

Serves 4-6

What a surprise! San Francisco food stylist Scotty McKinney's ice cream creation is rich, smooth, creamy and delicious—everything ice cream is supposed to be. Serve it with fresh fruit—a natural combination—or enjoy it just as it is.

Thoroughly combine in a blender:

> **4 egg yolks**
> **1 cup fromage blanc**
> **1 cup sugar**
> **1 cup whipping cream**

Follow general instructions for freezing in your ice cream maker.

ORANGE-ALMOND CREAM

Serves 8-10

Though reminiscent of Russian Pashka, this creamy dessert has a personality all its own. It is irresistably rich, cool and easy to prepare.

Have all ingredients at room temperature. Mix together thoroughly in a food processor or by hand:

> **1 pound (approximately 2 cups) fromage blanc**
> **1 navel orange, peeled and puréed**
> **1 teaspoon orange zest (colored outer rind of orange peel), grated**
> **2 ounces almond paste**
> **1 egg yolk**
> **1/2 cup unsalted butter**
> **1/3 cup sugar**

Line a ring mold, bowl or other interesting form with wet cheesecloth. Press the cheese mixture into the mold and refrigerate at least 4 hours and up to 24 hours. Unmold onto a serving platter and garnish with:

> **1/4 cup toasted slivered almonds**
> **sections from one mandarin orange, seeded**

CHOCOLATE CHÈVRE TART

Serves 8

Thanks to Kaye Henzerling, our local chocolate fanatic and dessert specialist, here is a tangy, chocolate tart with a rich cookie-like crust.

Preheat oven to 350º.

To prepare the crust for a 10-inch tart pan, cream by hand or in a processor:

1/2 cup unsalted butter, room temperature
1/2 cup sugar

Add:

1 egg yolk
1/2 cup ground almonds
1/2 teaspoon vanilla

Mix by hand until well blended, or process about 30 seconds.

Add:

1 cup flour

Work with your hands until smooth, or process until the dough forms a ball. Press dough into tart pan. Dough will be somewhat moist, so flour your hands.

Brush with:

1 lightly beaten egg white

Prebake the crust for 10 minutes at 350º. There is no need to weight the crust. It will rise somewhat but will not crack or form air bubbles. Prepare the filling while crust cooks and cools. In a double boiler, melt:

3 ounces semi-sweet chocolate

Set aside to cool. In a separate bowl or in a processor, beat until smooth but not runny:

2 cups fromage blanc

Add:

1/3 cup sugar
2 eggs
1 teaspoon vanilla
1 tablespoon rum
1 tablespoon cocoa

Beat or process until well blended. Add cooled, melted chocolate and beat again, quickly, to blend. Pour into prebaked shell and bake for 35-40 minutes at 350° or until set. Serve chilled.

If desired, decorate with:

whipped cream

This recipe can easily be adapted for a vanilla cheese tart with fresh fruit topping. Omit the cocoa and chocolate from filling and substitute amaretto for rum. Top the cooked tart with the following glaze:

1-1/2 cups sieved fresh fruit
1/2 cup sugar
1 tablespoon corn starch

Heat slowly until thickened and then cool. Glaze the tart and then top with fresh fruit.

STUFFED PEACH AND RASPBERRY SAUCE

Serves 6

The combination of tastes and textures in this preparation are unbeatable. This is a refreshing, light and satisfying end to any meal.

Peel, pit and poach:

6 ripe peach halves

    or

Drain:

6 canned peach halves

Crush to fine crumbs:

6 amaretti cookies (sold in colorful packages of 2 cookies each)

    or

1/4 cup almonds

Divide into 6 equal portions:

5 ounces very fresh chèvre (chabis or drained fromage blanc)

Roll each portion into a ball and roll each ball in the crumbs until well coated. Place a cheese ball into the pit section of each peach half. Place all the peach halves on a baking dish, carefully arranging them so as to not fall over. Heat them 8-10 inches under the broiler for 3-4 minutes until cheese and peaches are just warmed and the crumbs are crisped.

Spoon 3 tablespoons of raspberry purée onto each of 6 dessert plates. Place peach halves on raspberry purée. Drizzle with remaining purée.

Raspberry Purée:

Strain through a fine sieve:

1 pint of fresh or frozen raspberries

In a small saucepan combine the raspberry purée with:

3/4 cup sugar
1 tablespoon lemon juice

Bring mixture to a simmer and cook for 5 minutes, stirring constantly, or until purée is slightly thickened. Let cool.

TOURTEAU FROMAGER

Serves 8

So unlike cheesecakes we know in America, tourteau fromager has a texture similar to spongecake and a distinctive black top. It is a specialty of the Deux-Sèvres region of France. We eat it for breakfast or brunch, though it is delightful anytime.

In a processor or medium bowl, mix well:

1 cup flour
7 tablespoons butter
1 tablespoon oil
1/4 cup water
pinch of salt

Knead until well worked. The French throw the dough repeatedly against a work surface until elastic. Refrigerate for at least 30 minutes while preparing the filling.

Preheat the oven to 375°.

Separate:

4 eggs

Add to yolks:

3/4 cup sugar
1 teaspoon vanilla (optional)

Mix until thickened and somewhat white.

Add, and mix well:

5 ounces fresh chèvre (chabis)
4 tablespoons flour

Whip egg whites with a pinch of salt until stiff but not dry. Fold the whites into the yolk/cheese mixture. Remove the crust dough from the refrigerator and roll out large enough to line a one-quart brioche pan or a heatproof pyrex bowl. Place in the pan and trim edges. Pour filling into crust, forming a smooth rounded top. Bake at 375^0 for 45 minutes, then raise the temperature to 400^0 and bake for another 10-15 minutes. A knife inserted in the cake should come out clean and the top should be quite black and cracked. Serve the cake after it has cooled. Cook it the night before if you plan to serve it for breakfast or brunch.

FIGS WITH MINT CREAM

Serves 4

Here is a delightful and unusual light dessert.

In a food processor or blender mix thoroughly, 10-15 seconds:
> **2 tablespoons fresh mint, finely chopped**
> **1 tablespoon sugar**
> **3/4 cup fromage blanc**

Wash and dry:
> **8 fresh green or black figs**

Trim off stems.

Three serving suggestions:

1) Slice figs in half. Place four fig halves on each dessert plate. Use a pastry bag to decorate figs with cheese mixture.

2) Cut figs into a tulip shape by slitting each fig open in quarters from stem end to within a 1/2 inch from the bottom. Place two tulips on each dessert plate and a large dollop of cheese mixture into each fig center.

3) Cut figs into quarters. Arrange eight fig sections on each desert plate and allow guests to dip figs into a shared bowl of the cheese mixture.

PLUM COMPOTE

Serves 6

Freshness and simplicity are key to the elegance of this dessert. We used the luscious Santa Rosa plums but any red/purple variety will do.

In a saucepan, simmer over medium heat until thickened:
> **1 pound plums, pitted and quartered**
> **3/4 cup sugar**

Remove from heat and add:
> **juice of 1/2 lemon**

When ready to serve, prepare the fromage blanc. Mix briskly with a fork:
> **8 ounces (1 cup) fromage blanc**
> **1/4 cup heavy cream**
> **1-2 tablespoons sugar**

Serve compote slightly warm in individual bowls. Place one-sixth of cheese on each serving and sprinkle with:
> **1/4 cup toasted almond slivers**

Use any fruit in season, such as: berries, apples, apricots, peaches, or create your own fruit mixture.

WALNUT PIE

Serves 8-10

We tested this pie many times just for the joy of it. So sinfully rich, this is a suitable ending to a light meal. Or, if you want to be thoroughly decadent, serve as part of a holiday feast. The tart cheese and orange zest are a perfect counterpart to the buttery walnut filling.

Prepare the crust with a pastry cutter or a food processor:

1-1/2 cups flour
1/2 cup unsalted butter, chilled
2 tablespoons oil
1 tablespoon sugar
1/4 teaspoon salt

When the above mixture becomes the consistency of small peas, add:

2-4 tablespoons ice water

Mix, form into a ball, and refrigerate at least one hour.

Mix together in a small bowl:

1 egg
1/3 cup sugar
dash of salt
2 tablespoons melted butter
1/3 cup light corn syrup

When combined, stir in:

1-1/4 cups walnuts, chopped medium coarse
1/8 teaspoon vanilla

Remove crust from the refrigerator. Roll out to fit a 9 or 10-inch pie pan. Trim crust, and line the pan with aluminum foil, weight with 2 cups of beans or pie crust weights and prebake in 375⁰ oven for 10-15 minutes. Remove from oven, remove weights and pour the walnut mixture into the shell. Return to the oven and bake for 30 minutes.

Prepare the cheese mixture by lightly whipping:
> **1 pound (approximately 2 cups) fromage blanc**
> **1 tablespoon orange zest, grated or finely chopped**
> **1/3 cup sugar**
> **1 egg, lightly beaten**

When the walnut mixture has baked for 30 minutes, remove from oven and spread cheese mixture to cover walnuts. Smooth and swirl cheese. Return to oven and bake another 30-35 minutes. Serve when cooled.

RIVER CAFÉ STRAWBERRY CHÈVRE CAKE

Serves 8-10

Larry Forgione, of An American Place in New York, is known for his distinctive use of American products. Here is just one of his many unique creations using American goat cheese.

Hull, wash and leave whole:
> **2 pints large ripe strawberries**

Reserve 10 of the most beautiful berries. Make your own or buy:
> **one 10-inch Genoise cake**

Split into 2 layers. Mix together thoroughly:
> **1 pound (approximately 2 cups) fromage blanc**
> **1 cup fresh cream, whipped until stiff**
> **2 ounces honey**

Spread 1/4-inch thickness of above mixture over one layer of Genoise. Ring border of Genoise with all but the reserved 10 strawberries. Fill in around strawberries with remaining cheese and cream mixture. Top with second layer of Genoise. Cover thickly with:
> **1 cup fresh cream, whipped until stiff**

Decorate with the 10 reserved strawberries.

SWEET BEUREG

Serves 6-8

Dessert beuregs are twice the size of the savory ones in our STARTERS section, so for an elegant dessert, serve two per person. Follow the basic directions for working with the filo dough (page 33) but do not cut the dough in half lengthwise in the first step. Substitute one heaping tablespoon for the one teaspoon of filling per sheet.

For the sweet filling, mix in processor, or by hand, in medium bowl:
> **8 ounces very fresh chèvre (chabis, log or plain)**
> **2 eggs**
> **2 tablespoons fromage blanc or 2 tablespoons cream (fresh or sour)**
> **3 tablespoons sugar, or more to taste**
> **1 teaspoon cinnamon**
> **1/2 teaspoon vanilla (optional)**

Add:
> **1/4 cup raisins**
> **1/4 cup walnuts, chopped**

After all triangle packages have been formed, sprinkle top with:
> **white granulated sugar**

Bake in 400° oven for 15-20 minutes or until puffed and golden. Serve warm.

If blueberries are in season you may wish to substitute them (1/2 cup) for the raisins and walnuts.

SUMMER FRUIT WITH FROMAGE BLANC

Serves 6

The perfect ménage à trois of blackberries, peaches and goat fromage blanc makes summer in Sonoma County (or anywhere) even more special.

Peel and thinly slice:
> **6 fresh peaches**

Sort and pick through:
> **1-1/2 cups fresh blackberries**

Toss fruit in a bowl with:
> **2 tablespoons sugar or honey**
> **2 tablespoons brandy**

Let sit one hour at room temperature.

Mix together thoroughly:
> **8 ounces (1 cup) fromage blanc**
> **1/2 teaspoon lemon zest (colored outer rind of lemon peel), grated**
> **1/4 teaspoon vanilla**
> **1/4 cup sugar**

Beat until stiff:
> **2 egg whites**
> **1 teaspoon sugar**
> **pinch of salt**

Gently fold beaten egg whites into cheese mixture. Divide fruit into 6 dessert bowls. Top each with one-sixth of the above mixture.

Sprinkle evenly with:
> **1/4 cup ground walnuts, toasted.**

SOME MORE IDEAS . . .

Mix softened unsalted butter with sugar and fromage blanc. Serve with fruits that have been marinated in kirsch.

Roll a white chèvre log (do not use the ash-coated logs) in orange zest; wrap in plastic and store in the refrigerator 2-3 days. Serve slices with crisp sugar cookies for dessert, or serve with croissants for a delightful breakfast. The longer you leave the logs in the refrigerator, the stronger the orange flavor.

Mix fromage blanc with lightly whipped cream, sugar, and rum to taste. Mound on bananas that have been sliced once, lengthwise. Sprinkle liberally with chopped nuts.

Substitute goat cheese for cottage cheese in blintze fillings, or sweeten fromage blanc and roll in crêpes. Serve with jam.

For dessert, breakfast, teatime, or any time, warm walnut bread and goat cheese make an excellent combination.

Slice chabis, warm in the oven, arrange in a pool of chocolate sauce on a dessert plate, and sprinkle with chopped walnuts. Decadent!